A WANDSWORTH BOY'S JOURNEY
THROUGH LIFE

by

JAMES G PARKER

For my children, Jackie, Colin, Janine;
and for Maggie making the third part come true

The Life and Times of a Wandsworth Kid

(As remembered but mostly as told by Joyce)

I was born in St. James's hospital Balham SW19 in the early hours of January 16th 1939 to Emily Maud Parker nee Carney married to one Albert Edward Parker. Mum was 31 and dad 37. The world in Europe was at war and we were soon to follow. I was blissfully unaware of this of course, although I would be soon enough. Mother was the only daughter of James and Maud Carney: younger sister to James and elder to Frederick. Both these grand-parents figured largely in my life. Dad's parents were deceased.

Mother was an attractive woman and dad courted her in the laundry in Streatham where they both worked. Mainly by pestering her at every opportunity. Mum wasn't overly attracted to Dad but persistence won the day and they were married at Wandsworth Register Office on Christmas Eve 1929. Joyce came along in 1930 and enjoyed free reign as an only child until I put in an appearance..

Mum, then, was laundress and dad a maintenance engineer. If he was needed he was to be found in the pub opposite. The boss never complained because he was in there too! They lived in Acacia road Streatham. War had come and coming out the Anderson shelter one night to find the house gone.(bombed). Mum decided to leave him and went off to live with her mother. Reconciliation came after Mum suffered a nasty road accident on her bicycle involving tram lines and a lorry at Tooting. While in hospital the authorities tracked down dad fearing she wasn't going to make it. Lucky for me, eh?

She never really loved dad: you've made your bed, lie on it. So along came me much to Joyce's delight in a baby brother. Then realised. I was the new centre of attention rather took the icing off the Gingerbread.

I was raised I suppose, after a couple of false starts on the Henry Prince Estate off the Garratt Lane between Wandsworth and Tooting, We lived in three different flats due to Mother's penchant for moving every couple of years. But for most of it was the ground floor flat 241 from early years until eleven when we moved across to 256 on the top floor. I was evacuated with mum to Three Bridges. Joyce went off somewhere else. Dad insisted mum returned when he realised she was helping a woman run a cafe whose biggest customers were the local Army lads. The next evacuation found us in Buxton but the place was alive with Fleas. Mum said she'd sooner risk the bombs and we returned to the Henry Prince, The fleas were sorted with a toothbrush dipped in Paraffin as in Paraffin Oil. Head scrubbed, then washed. It worked. I was vaccinated while evacuated. Mothers were offered a cup of tea while the process was carried out.

The flats have changed somewhat and 241 is now No. 49 St Johns road.

THE WAR YEARS

My most vivid memories even now was hearing the Air Raid Siren and being pulled from my bed, a snatch of stars and the unique smell of the shelter which was just outside the Flats. The drone of unsynchronised aircraft engines. We synchronised ours Jerry didn't. Took me years to get over the feeling of apprehension on hearing aircraft overhead. Once the All Clear went we could return home. One night coming out the shelter saw the local Catholic Church ablaze having suffered a direct hit. All our flat windows were blown in and I insisted someone go in and get my tooth fairy money: I was saving for a kaleidoscope. (half a crown). The MOD factory across the Wandle was hit one night in an incendiary raid. They had a huge Barrage Balloon anchored close by too! Finding Shrapnel was good as was trying to relight incendiary bombs quite small things.

We lived on The Henry Prince Estate ground floor flat No. 241 having moved down from a top floor of the long central block. There were eight flats in our block and opposite us was Mrs Knowles, a very ancient creature. She kept Goats in hers. Above was Lil Dartnel and opposite of all things a Belgian family. Whatever next? Over them were the Prestwitches. I was sweet on Rosemarie and we courted and argued in all innocence over the years. Then Mr Kerner. He had a motor-cycle combination. The only vehicle in the street. Later in life he would take us kids up to the London museums on a Sunday. Great fun! Top floor Mrs Step and her six girls. And finally Dorothy Armatige. Though they may have come after the Belgians went home. I thought she was stuck-up.

We called the estate 'the buildings'. Mum, Dad, my big sister Joyce bro Michael and bro Arp, Oh and me. The flat had three bedrooms, lounge, kitchen, bathroom, toilet, coal cellar. There was a bath in the bathroom alongside which was a large gas copper. One filled the copper from the tap over it. Lit the gas and waited for it to get hot. More water and the overflow pipe filled the bath. Simple. The only sink was in the kitchen. That was used for everything. It had an Ascot water heater over it which lit on turning on the water. You only heated what you used. (money was tight). This was also reflected in the food. Nothing was wasted. Hence bubble and squeak to use the taters and greens left over and even if Mum made a Spotted Dick pudding the leftovers were sliced and fried. Love grub. Toast and dripping which was the rendered fat and meat jelly. Plenty of salt with it too. There were no fridges. The butcher had one but not in our neck of the woods. To save the milk going off, mum would boil it. Trouble was when it cooled it formed a skin: bit like custard. But the skin was whisked into it. I hated it. If you were really short mum would make up a bundle of old clothes and I'd take them round to the recycle lady in Wardley Street. Huge shapeless woman with a huge pair of scales. She'd give you a few coppers for your trouble. The Cat, Henry had a Whiting from the wet fish shop opposite. That was dropped on the kitchen floor under the sink until it was merely a head the replaced with a.n. other.

The river Wandle ran behind the buildings and that was great for games and exploring. There was a green field of sorts; the bomb debris which included what was left of the Catholic Church and the Neptune drinks factory. We'd collect Lead from the electric cables and melt it down in a tin and pour it into the frog of a brick. Can't think why? It was also the place we acted out what we'd seen at the pictures. Tarzan. Hopalong Cassidy. Heroes all. The Step girls taught me skipping. And rounders and hopscotch were other pastimes. Dad was now a stoker at the Wandsworth Gas works. Mum was variously a theatre cleaner or cook up in London.

My mate John Richards whom I met at school would go up to Ravenscroft park where there was a large lake. Always an attraction. fishing for tiddlers, sailing bits of boats. And there was a wooded area for playing Indians or whatever. One had to watch out for men exposing themselves. Bit like the pictures. All boys wore shorts until age eleven and secondary school. While sitting in the pictures a man would sit alongside with a raincoat which would be draped over ones legs and a hand would find it's way up the leg of one shorts. We soon learned to vacate the seat when this happened. I even had one man follow me out to the toilet and sucked my cock. I was off home like a scalded cat. Couldn't tell mother; be another good hiding. As we're talking pictures. At the end of the show (last Film) they would play the National Anthem and you were expected to stand for.

Once we got a bit bigger and had bikes of sorts. Wimbledon Common. George Atherton another school pal insisted looking for Caesar's well. Said we'd found it but I was highly dubious. It was his job in life to make a botanist of me and insisted I learn the plants and the trees. There were more lakes or meres on the Common and more men exposing themselves. One just ignored it or cycled off somewhere else. A go cart was a wizz if you could lay your hands on some pram wheels, other than that it was rounders, hopscotch or skipping with the girls.

The Summer might find the neighbours sitting out on the 'garden' wall. One woman was forever threading cotton/string through what looked like socks with no foot. They were destined to be Gas Mantles. Yes Joyce had gas lighting at Hazelrigg road.

SCHOOL YEARS

I started at Wandle school at age four. Mum lied about my age. I wasn't consulted. As well as dinners they also did 'teas' at 2d a pop. A boon to busy Mums. My mate Donald suggested spending it on sweets was a better idea which I thought was great until reported back to mother. Another good hiding. Off would come her slipper or anything else close to hand. Anyway the Wandle got bombed and we were up to the infants on Magdalen road. A couple of classrooms. Miss Painter and Mrs Oldroyd. My peg had a picture of a Dinghy over it and I sat next to Kate in glasses and pigtails.

We seemed to learn to read in no time and wend our way home through the cemetery which bordered Magdalen road reading the gravestones. We had a conjurer one Christmas and I won the Tommy-gun off the Christmas tree. In wood with a super clacker. Miss Painter told us she was getting married and would be called.?? I don't remember. I hope she had a good life!

Tranmere road Primary School

I don't remember the first class master but I did get my bottom slapped for high spirits in the playground. Mr Calverley was next he would sometimes digress and tell us tales of the Crusades. I spent two years with him as they had discovered my true age. Bit of a waste of space really. Then to Mr Brown who taught in the overspill huts at the back of the playground. No we only used one floor of the school. He suffered from Alopecia. And after a parents visit by mother I found myself taking in parcels of Black market tea that mother got from uncle Con at thirty pence a pop and two and a half for me.

We had a man visit and all sat on the floor in the hall while he told us of tales of derring do from when he served with T.E. Lawrence. We also had a Canadian teacher come and we feared he'd use the word bum. What a more innocent and homogeneous age!

I did well in the eleven plus and was selected for the Elliott that was a Central school. Between the Grammar and the secondary modern and said farewell to my then lifelong friend John Richards who with Bruce Denton went to a secondary modern in Tooting.

I enjoyed the Elliott. It was a school of long tradition having been started by an ex Indian Colonel. First two years I was in Mr Hoffman's class. Always puzzled me how a German should be teaching so soon after the war. But he was a good teacher. After that in the third year it was Ted Edwards class. I really liked Ted We were now streamed. Parents were advised that their son was more suited to a technical/commercial education Tech boys did woodwork, metalwork, tech drawing etc. Commercial boys typewriting, bookkeeping, etc. I did tech. We all did Art Geog and games. Once a year the Cross Country was held on Wimbledon Common. All boys will run; no excuse tolerated. I was 247th out of 280 but made 47th next run. The school motto was Manners Mayketh Man. There was a large Frieze around the hall painted by the art master Mr Mills. We were taken to the Granada Tooting where the London Sinfonia played us a selection of the classics while the conductor explained each piece. To the Old Vic, and a production of Macbeth. There was a day in January of 53 when there was a hush over the school, or at least among the pupils. They were hanging in Wandsworth prison. He and Accomplice Graig had a burglary go wrong and a copper was shot dead by Craig. Bentley took the rap! And of course when the King George VI died, Mr Morgan broke the news in the gravest of terms. On a lighter note. The beak Mr James came in class and informed us that a new pupil would be starting. Name of Christie. He suffered a lisp. Woe betide any boy found ribbing him for the lisp. Heads would roll. In the event Christie was a good footballer and was taken to by all.

I would normally come top in class. Was in the school choir and the swimming gala and the school play produced by Mr Edwards. Mr Hook the Geography master took us in his Triumph Mayflower at sixty miles and hour down the Robin Hood Way to Ted's house for a celebratory meal. And a treasure hunt with a £1 prize. I left at fifteen years of age. Dad being increasingly ill and mum needed my input to the family finances however small.

DIVERSIONS

Mother! Go over the Chippie/laundry and get my whatever. You were never served as a child until all the adults had been. Here's a shilling, go to the barbers you and your two brothers. Three short back and sides and tuppence for Molyneaux. There were three chairs and one in a corner. He in the corner never stopped talking. Virtually held court. One would count the men in there to find one's place. Remembering who came in also. As well as a haircut one could have shave (cut-throat razor) hot towels and the hair removed from ones ears with a lighted taper. Ah my turn. No! Sit down boy; come along sir your next. It used to infuriate me. Sixty odd years later I still have my hackles rise on being held up in a shop.

Shopping for mum's errands wasn't so bad. David Griegs, Home and Colonial. They stored dry goods in sacks on the floor. Sugar was weighed loose from the sack and poured into a blue bag. Likewise dried peas. Sainsbury's next door found you queuing at one counter for eggs, bacon, cheese and the across to the other one for your tea, coffee and jams. The chemist sold iron filings, Sulphur and Potassium which was handy for making fireworks Nearly blinded myself on one occasion.

One of mum's other devices to get us out from under her feet on a Sunday was Sunday school, which put us in the church choir. Vicar John sacked Mike and I for messing about. The other diversion was to hand me three sixpences for the bus fare to the end of Mitchum Common. Come back through the common: ponds to inspect, golf course for hunting balls and all the other pursuits of children. When you run out of common I'd three threepenny bits for the fare home. Mum would have dinner ready, followed by a good wash and bed. If I sat real quiet while mum was listening to the radio I might get another half hour. I used to read in bed anyway. Had a torch under the covers.

HOLIDAYS

Mum was a great one for a day out, or a week away. We did go Hop picking once. One lived in a little tin shed and cooked on a fire outside. Picked hops all day for whatever they paid. Mike and I were far more interested in the Ladybirds and Arthur was far too young to take any interest. So after a couple of days we came home. Days out on a charabanc were always good. Brighton, Hastings. Dad booked us to Basingstoke one time and mum had to pay the driver to take us on to Bournemouth. Well it sounds like seaside resort!

Then it was a caravan in a farmers field at East Wittering. That was brilliant. Trouble was the outside loo was full of bloody great spiders. Ugh! mum would say to me,the beach is that way; across the stubble field. I'll be down later with the others. We'd have a week and Joyce and Ron would come down the second week and I would stay on with them. Must have been a bind having your young brother stay with you when you were newly wed. Well, sort off. There were pictures in the village hall on Saturdays 6d (two and a half pence) entry and you waited between reel changes. No sweets or ice creams. Magic stuff though. A bit later in life we'd go to the Isle of Sheppey and a chalet at Leysdown The local amusement arcade would give you thirteen pennies for your shilling. You can win but you can't beat the game. Mum played Bingo and we played the slots with our shilling and had fish and chips on the way back. Simple pleasures. Another diversion on a Sunday was to get a bus to Putney and walk the tow-path to Hammersmith. We'd have ice creams at Putney and dad a pint at Hammersmith. Through Johnny Coleman we got involved with a schoolmaster who liked to take children on holiday. One trip we had was the IoW Camping. Bell tents, canvas washstands and loos across the field. trips out were organised out depending how much money mum and dad had supplied. Mike and I did most of the trips. Can't remember Arthur being there. I did make firm friends with a boy there and we were both quite cut up come parting. Another of I Wackham's (as he referred to himself) was camping in the woods at Oxshott On the last day he asked for volunteers to stay and help dismantle the tents. Muggings volunteered. He spent the evening in the local pubs feeding me crisps and lemonade. About the third pub a copper came over and spoke to me. He'd noticed me outside several pubs. Thus he went in and had a word with old Whackem. Must have frightened him fartless because we had a quiet night and I was away first thing. Mother was horrified when I told her. Now I understand why!

FAMILY LIFE

Joyce had been courting Ron for a while. Met at a dance

at the local Town Hall. He was always sending me out for bottles of Lemonade. Probably to get me out of the way for half hour or so. They were married in St. Andrews church in the Garratt lane and all the family came. Uncle John Aunt Emma, a barrel of beer was set up. I tried that; tasted horrible. Once it was all over it was down to me to fill up the old pram with the empties and walk them all the way back to Speke road Battersea. There was a deposit on the bottles. (natural recycling) Couple of three miles. There was a lot less traffic then. Dad worked at the Gas works in Wandsworth as a stoker, although the boiler was oil fired. I did go with him one time to light the bloody thing, Once lit dad realised the water feed pipes were frozen. Panic! Solved by soaking rags in Naptha and wrapping the pipes and igniting them. Worked. If Mum wasn't cleaning theatres in Drury Lane she was cooking. Kensington Palace, Buckingham Palace (staff). The local Home for Incurables. She'd say to me. That bit of Lamb left over from Sunday. Put it through the mincer with a slice of bread half an Onion and a pinch of Sage. Mash the spuds and do a Cottage Pie. Oh and an egg custard. Should have grown up as Jamie Oliver. Thought about being a chef.

Mum had taken a job locally on a punch machine. (work was easily found in those days) anyway she managed to punch a hole in her thumb. Must have hurt. She got forty pounds compensation which went on a nine inch Bush Bakelite television. We watched the Coronation of the Queen with half the estate crowded into our flat.

I went camping with Ginger Hull. He was a lad I walked to school with once we'd moved to flat 256. We were about twelve; had a tent of sorts and we camped out Chertsey way. Proper camping ground. We had a Primus stove that was temperamental to say the least. It had an Asbestos plate affair which sat over the flame and we could make toast. Seemed to live on the stuff if I remember correctly. We did go scrumping one night but the owner called the

Police having heard us and we were chased out of there. Bruce Denton's brother turned up out the blue looking for a place to spend the night. Trading on the fact that Bruce and I had been friends he shared the tent and my sleeping bag and was then trying to bugger me at the same time! I never did like the bastard. He went the next day and we continued to swim in the river and generally mess about. A great storm of rain proved the inadequacy of the tent and we packed up and went home. The next adventure with Ginger was to cycle to Southampton to see his sister. Ginge sorted the route which I now know was down the A3 to Cosham and then along the A27 to Sot'on. Long trip. Stopped by the Punch Bowl and had a large Orange. Made it to his sisters and on return in the dark about Staines were stopped by a copper as I had no rear light. Decent bloke lent me a battery which I had to return on pain of death. (his).

Yes we were quite tired on return. But it wasn't uncommon for me to take off on my bike to the coast. John Richards and I did Brighton first. Another favourite was visiting airfields. We would lie on the tarmac at Croydon outside the terminal as the passengers came out to board the D.H.Rapide that was sitting there. Heathrow was another. John, Bruce and I down the Great West Road, three abreast on the cycle path. Heathrow then was little more than a few Nissan huts some ranch fencing and a bit of a runway. John and I also went across to Blackbushe and were looking at all the Mosquito's that were stored there until a policeman came puffing over on his bike and moved us on. Bruce faded out of the picture but John and I stayed close. Swimming was our great passion. and we would visit various baths from Latchmere's 'penny nakeds' (literally) boys only. The pool next door was sixpence. Fulham was our favourite but I can't remember why.

Going round to John's in Cargill road one met a man in a brown pin stripe suit hanging about the corner and further down a man in a Black Homburg and Camel haired coat standing about. He was the local bookie. Gambling was verboten off course and betting shops never existed. On occasion Mum would send me round to him with a piece of paper with her horses and a couple of bob. And my visit to the pictures depended on Snowdrop or Brown Rascal coming home! Mind you it was take your brother Arthur. Mum. He's only six and I'm a whole ten!

CHRISTMAS

One's letter to Santa outlining all one's hopes for presents was written and solemnly placed on the coal shovel and wafted up the chimney. Decorations were hand made. Gummed strips of coloured paper were licked to form a ring and interlaced with others for the 'chain'. Crepe paper would be cut into strips and cross folded to form another 'garland'. Mum would make the cake and we'd all have a stir and make a wish. Nuts which only appeared at this time of the year would be cracked in the door. Likewise Tangerines and new copper coins also only appeared about now!

DAD

Never really knew the man. He was the figure in a flat cap that smelt of tars oils and tobacco. Usually asleep in the armchair. He'd been in the workhouse as a child but never mentioned it, even if we walked past the place. His shifts at the gasworks earned him at the time. £9 for the 6-2 shift. £11 for the 2-10 shift and £13 for the night shift. Liked a pint. Didn't seem to have any friends to speak of. Was proud of his family and jealous of mother. They rowed a lot.

MUM

Kept it all together I suppose. Dished out love and punishment as required. Fed and watered us. Taught the mores of society and pushed and cajoled us as and loved and comforted us when sick or unwell. She never took a drink except maybe Christmas when she'd have a Milk Stout. She died in '74 over fond of the VP Wine.

HEALTH

We had our ups and downs. I got Meningitis and was whisked off to Thornton Heath and fancy I can still remember the Lumbar Punch. I contracted Scarlet Fever and was taken to Hither Green by ambulance and put in isolation. I was eight. Was over the bitter Winter of forty-seven/eight. While there I got every other childhood disease probably from climbing out the fire escape and visiting other wards. Eventually Mother simply took me away. I had my Tonsils taken out at St. Thomas's and was sent for convalescence. They gave me a wheel chair to get around in. I could only reach the tyres. Watched all the ole boys and their Rolls Razors; and the nurse in all seriousness. Have your Bowels been opened today? Must have been April as I picked a huge bunch of Bluebells for mum to take home. If I wasn't in, then brother Mick was. He dived over a wall on the estate onto a broken toilet pedestal and tore the flesh from his middle finger. Home to mum, wrapped in a towel and into a pram and across to A&E at St James, Balham They sewed his finger to his thigh to help the flesh regrow. He has a hairy middle finger centre to this day.

Mum went in with a Duodenal Ulcer which was operated on by a top surgeon who had just returned from holiday. I remember mum telling all and sundry. Dad suffered with Chronic Bronchitis. Dr Lee would prescribe Gee's linctus (no connection). Dad had bottles of the stuff.

Looked like cold tea and was about as effective. Dad smoked roll ups but everyone smoked in those days. Worked in the Gas works. Stoker! You tell me. Medicine didn't seem to have come far from Leeches and bleeding people. Dad was in and out of hospital and there was no dole or sick pay in those days. A bit if you were on the panel. Thus we moved from the 'posh' flats in Iron Bridge road to a place in the Queenstown road Battersea. A three up sharing a common doorway. I had to leave school at fifteen with no exams to help with the family finances. At least I could contribute a bit. On medical advice we moved to the south coast for the sea air. Denmead flats in Gresham street Portsmouth. Didn't do dad any good; his constant complaint about a burning pain in his abdomen, was met with the reply: it's from the constant coughing from the smoking. He begged them to open him up and at least have a look. But No! The profession knew best. Dad died in the QA Portsmouth of haemorrhage from Gastric ulcers. Poor man was fifty-three. I was going to sea for a career and his last words to me were. Beware the painted ladies. Whatever did he mean? I found out eventually.

WORK

My first job apart from papers and bakers boy was a gofer at Kemsleys Newspapers in the Grays Inn road. You were sent round to other newspapers/magazines with pictures or other printing material. Buses or taxis as appropriate. I soon learned to use my bike. Going up by train with a carriage full of men in pin stripes, bowler hats and rolled brollies which were de-rigeur was too much for me. So flying round London: Fleet street and the surrounds. Claimed for buses. One also got Luncheon Vouchers as part of ones pay. These helped subsidise one's lunch or could even be traded on. Quite successful things; taken everywhere. I spent a spell with a man whose job was to check the correct adverts had appeared in the papers. and one late night he sent me down to the print room for a paper or two and thus I had tomorrows paper today.

I had a daft idea that I might be a press photographer and I was moved to Mr Stillers dept which was photography. The Queen at the time was doing a commonwealth tour and was then in Gibraltar. Photos would appear from the slot in the development lab and someone would type out a caption: as The Queen meeting the Lord Lieutenant, Barbary Apes etc. I would then duplicate them on a Gestener duplicator which was all inky carbons. I was not allowed to place the captions until I had been shown. Dozens would be produced and I'd leg it round the various news establishments with them. Then there was odd jobs. Mr Stiller. Take this registered letter up the P.O. Mount Pleasant was just up the road and off I went and duly posted same. On return he wanted a receipt. Receipt? I posted it. He went bananas and sent me back to retrieve it. Well I'd never seen a Registered letter before. In truth I probably wasn't taking too much notice. So that was the end of that job. In my defence Mr Stiller didn't keep his boys too long.

Job Centre. What do you want to do? There's a job here learning to be a Plant fitter or another assembling electric hair clippers. I fancy that, I want to do electrical work. That was at 215 Putney Bridge road. Converted house. Machine shop ground floor. Assembly/repair upstairs and the bedrooms as offices. Wally Pratt was the foreman and I assembled Clukes clippers or Whal England clippers. Loved it. Small friendly place. Annual beano as it was called was to Southend on sea and the Kursall. Had a great day. The firm was doing a promotion and they took on another lad. We took a weekend to visit his grandmother in Banbury by bike. Left late and had to doss down in her shed with a pig until daybreak. Can't remember owt else about it.

Then out of the blue mother said to me. Your out of that job I've got you an interview with the Post Office at Waterloo. Trainee telephone engineer. But Mum! No argument, mum said. The 'job' was a two year learnership as a y2yc on telephone systems. Six months on the Exchange, then Line work plus plus. We also got two days at school as war babies we'd missed a lot of teaching. That was the thinking by the powers that be. I finished up in the Exchange at Waterloo where the engineers sat. They gave me some tools in particular a pair of pliers with the insulation worn away and I was always getting electric shocks from the 50volts they used to run the place. Never thought to tape them up. No formal training but I was learning. Then one day I was called before the big boss. Office, desk etc. I understand young man that you intend to go to sea. (Granddads influence). well yes   when I'm sixteen. Well what are you doing here? Mum said! You will tender your resignation effective whenever and leave. All a bit heavy handed for a fifteen year old. Job shop. No unemployment benefit, you resigned. I was pushed. Having explained, we were agreed. Anyway it was time to begin the interviews for the National Sea Training schools. On an interview at the Shipping Federation on Leadenhall Street an August body of men (three), asked me questions like how to mend a puncture. I passed and was sent to NSTS Sharpness for ten weeks training. Funny the courts would offer yobs six months Borstal or go to sea. No interviews there!

So Paddington to Neath. Spend four hours at Neath all of twenty-five yards long and nothing but nothing else waiting for the local train to Sharpness, Met and escorted to the regulating office for induction and huts assignment. We had arrived to start our new life.

NATIONAL SEA TRAINING SCHOOL, SHARPNESS.

SEA SCHOOL

The huts accommodated about thirty boys in two tier bunks, no linen. Blankets only. Concrete construction. Ablutions block between. All training was done aboard the ship in classrooms of sorts. One of the boys who had been there some time said to me: learn a couple of knots and they'll make you a bosun's mate first test. Basically the idea was to teach us parts of a ship. Names of sail and their parts. Leech, clew, cringle. The compass etc. So when we eventually found ourselves aboard ship we wouldn't be complete novices. i.e. at least we'd know the language. Ahoy me hearties. We soon settled in and quickly found out there wasn't enough to eat. There was a cafe down the road where one could get tea and a wad. Most of us never had the money for that either. On a Thursday we collected our dole money, say £1.50 can't remember the exact amount. Having signed for it at table one you moved to table two where they took most of it off you to pay for the uniform. There was Dungaree type things, a wooly pully and a blouson with shoulder flashes saying Mercantile Marine. So what monies were left didn't run to many tea and wads down the cafe: and for the smokers among us life was desperate. Fortunately I didn't. A lad opposite would reach for his in the morning before his eyes were opened and go into a paroxysm of coughing like my ole dad. Put me off fags for life! Compass, a lad from Luton who should have been doing a Stewards course but because he stood in the wrong queue on arrival was to be a deckie. No they wouldn't correct the error. He couldn't 'box' a compass hence the moniker. He'd wash in the morning fully dressed hands only.

The ablutions block was divided down the centre by a long galvanised trough, further divided along it's length and the sub divided into sinks surmounted by hot and cold taps. Toilets running along the walls behind. On morning instead of marching us down to class the instructor stopped at the ablutions block. Right he say. Strip! Strip? In front of you and all these boys? Strip we did. Fill the sinks with warm water and splash it over yourselves and thus you bathe. Once we'd got over our shyness we did it for fun! The smooth soapy concrete floors made lovely slides.

I learned my knots and was made a bosun's mate and promptly put in charge of our hut. Come Saturday, parade, inspection us then billets. Bosun's mates were issued with six boys and a tin of polish to clean and polish hut and floors. Have you tried to get six boys to polish floors? We did discover with two sitting on the end of a blanket on the floor and being pulled two other lads was a great way to shine floors. Right 11a.m. and the Captain and his officers are doing inspections. All lined up in hut doorway. Chas appears. Can you hide me I escaped the parade and now nowhere to hide. As everyone else is legitimately lined up, we put him in a tall metal locker. Just before the Captain appears Chas falls through the locker floor. No time for anything stuff him in another: hold on to a hook or something. Kittens for me during inspection. We got away with it. Who'd be a bosun's mate? There was another diversion in the cinema at Dursley but the effort of getting there and back rather took the icing of the gingerbread.

We were also approached by the Royal Navy re joining the Royal Naval Reserve. Day out in Bristol 'all expenses paid' while your processed. Seemed a good idea at the time so went for it. We also had a lecture from a doctor about consorting with women of easy virtue. What's he on about? The doc said some of you would put your cocks where I'd hesitate to put my walking stick. Ah! We couldn't wait. Once we'd completed our six weeks sea training we were retained for camp maintenance. Digging allotments. Grass cutting. I remember one Acto machine like on oversize barbers clippers; all open teeth at the front being operated by sixteen year olds. H&E would have a fit today. But we survived. All in all it was good fun It was Summer and the Sun shone. Swimming in the canal was allowed and we were not over supervised when off classes.

Once all that was over I was issued with a seaman's discharge book in which would be entered ones ship, voyages and conduct and rating. A Seaman's Identity card complete with photo and fingerprints thereon. I was officially in the Mercantile Marine. I was sweet on a girl just up from us on the Queenstown road and we went for a walk in Battersea Park. Me in my 'uniform' with it's shoulder flashes, We were skirting the pond and the Park Ranger asked me. Have you been out yet? I thought he meant boating on the lake. Er, no I say! Well when you do get yourself a bit of black ham, making the classic arm gesture. Can't beat it!

Funny enough my first port of call was Portsmouth to start my four weeks RNR training. Report to HMS Dido on the North Wall in the dockyard.

We began by being kitted out as befitting sailors and given in to the gentle care of a petty officer to groom us in the ways of the RN. We were about ten or twelve if memory serves. Two weeks learning how to salute. Ranks and badges and marching on Whale Island.

HMS DIDO

HMS THESEUS

Then issued with rail warrants for Rosyth to join HMS Theseus.

This was a light fleet carrier and again we were assigned a P.O. We continued to learn how the Navy did things. Slept in Hammocks in a 'mess'. Most mornings were spent cleaning guns. Boat drill. Learning to row. The navy call it; pulling. And Theseus was travelling down the coast, showing the flag. A run ashore in Scarborough had ladies saying: touch your collar for luck sailor. I tried a pint of Tetleys bitter as recommended by Leeds. (a Yorkshire lad). Thought it was horrible. I got into a punch-up with another over one of the lads. Me his knight in shining armour, and, though we were soon separated I found the victim playing with my cock under the table at the next lecture. A sort of thank you I suppose. Never did it again.

More trouble. Captains rounds and I'm the man presenting the 'mess'. Come on Leeds stop playing cards there's an inspection due. The marine bugler steps through the door and Leeds is lying on deck with fifty-two cards spilt all over him. The captain Alastair Mars immediately all concern for Leeds. Next day I'm on Jankers for failing to present the place properly. I got to fire my first weapon on board, A Lee Enfield modified to be a 22. We fired at targets under the lifts. Turned out to be a good shot. We finished in Weymouth and had a week there before being discharged. The idea was that we would do two weeks every year to keep ones hand in. In the event I never did another day.

DOCK STREET

Living in London when I began sea training I was assigned to Dock Street in the east end. Out at Aldgate east across and down Lehman street to Dock street. There was a public convenience in Lehman street and when you paid your penny to the attendant he open the door and polished the seat. The original reason to charge a penny.

The shipping office was as a Post Office with a wire counter, scuffed bare wooden floor and men hanging about. With some trepidation I handed over my discharge book and asked for a job. Right Lad Tremorvah, Swansea upstairs see the doc and back here for a railway warrant sharpish. It was the usual drop them and cough routine. Ten seconds. Right lad here's your warrant. Report tomorrow M.V. Tremorvah Swansea docks. And that was it. No explanations just get on with it. Gave me time to go home and pack.

Paddington to Swansea and I found my way to the docks and the ship. It was early afternoon. A man met us on board and showed me a cabin. (certified three boys). and get myself forrard sharpish. He wanted a hand stowing stores. Paint etc., I found later it was Mr. Palin the Bosun. One of the other sailors whom I met said don't do any work your not signed on yet. The process began the following day with the various officials in the officers mess. One presented one's discharge book. Deck boy £7.50 a month; sign articles here and you were a member of the crew, They signed a Radio Officer on before me. £3 a month. In those days Marconi employed all radio officers. So this was a token pay from the company. Probably supplied the radio kit too.

So work began. There was me. Larry, and Norman as boys. All first trippers. About twelve on deck. Four or five engineers. Five firemen and a donkeyman. Three stewards, bosun, chippie. Captain and three mates and apprentii. Oh and two cooks. Head chef being known as Doc. We spent some time in Swansea cleaning up the ship then sailed round to Thames Haven to load cement for Kenya. Great excitement sailing up the channel and gazing at the land in the distance. Stop staring get back to work. Ouch! We were to load 10.00 tons of cement in 1cwt bags.

The bags came down on a conveyor belt and were lifted off by two men and placed in a cargo sling and winched aboard. Took some days I cannot remember how long, and then it was batten down the hatches. Slip the dock and away. Next stop Port Said. Egypt. The work on the ship was to wash all the dust and cement off using deck hoses. Bit like a fireman. Then to Suji (Wash) the paintwork, deck heads and bulwarks Chip the deck of rust using chipping hammers and re-paint using the bosun's black concoction with a wad of cotton waste. There was also a bone of contention. One of us boys had to be peggy! A term from when a sailor who had lost a leg could only be useful in the galley or mess as a waiter. One was supposed to collect the meals from the dumb waiter and serve the deck crew and the bosun and chippie. Wash up and stow. Of course as a youth it rankled. I'd had to do enough at home. But no choice, Larry fell to it with a will and was polishing the copper urn and cleaning the place. He was right really and once we'd settled into it, it wasn't so bad. The dumb waiter broke and one then had to leg it up to the galley for the grub, Me being me and having heard it somewhere and sat in the galley waiting repeated. Who called the cook a twat? Who called the twat a cook? Doc was making Yorkshire pudding at the time and I got smeared a faceful. One should consider ones words. They were a young crowd as the deck crew were generally known And were everlastingly exposing themselves and asking us boys to play with them. Or bent over doing deck work would find a fingers jabbed up one's arse and the cry. Hows that for centre? I hated it. A fireman who had brought a film developing kit as a do it in a cannister style of thing. Asked me to help him operate it. No problem, but he was only after buggering me and was more than difficult to stop him. Filthy old Sod.

TREMORVAH OFF CAPE TOWN

Egypt and the Canal

And suddenly we were off Port Said. Once we'd anchored we were surrounded by bum boats. Floating markets. Egyptians came aboard to sell their wares. Lighters, watches, cut-throat razors, scissors, playing cards and rag books containing the most explicit pornography. Words not pictures. Don't buy a watch, once the 'cricket' dies it's finished. Referring to the tick that watches had in them days. While there and I don't know how an Egyptian told me my fortune, reading my palm. Your life he said is divided roughly roughly into three parts. First part not very special, second part much the same. (oh thanks very much). Third part best of all. You will never have any money. You will never be broke and you will know much love. Sickness comes three times. That was about it. Funny he never mentioned children.

Once there were enough ships to form a convoy we set off with a pilot on board through the Suez Canal. Standing on the deck I couldn't reach the shore with a thrown potato. The convoy proceeded to the Bitter Lakes where the Northbound convoy was held and thus we passed on and down to Port Tewfiq and out into the Red Sea. Travelling down the Red Sea we encountered a swarm of Locusts which would blunder into one. Quite a sight all greeny pink. Ugh! Especially half way up the mast. Soon passed however much to my relief. The weather became hot and in fact there are two islands at the bottom end of the Red sea called the Gates of Hell. We bunkered in Aden passing the barren rocks of Aden. 'Mountains' rising straight out the sea. The ship burnt about ten tons of fuel oil a day. Larry was the son of a RAF family and said his brother was serving in Aden. Managed to find his brother and equipping ourselves with swim trunks joined him on the RAF type beach for swimming. We also racked up in the NAAFI later and overdosed on beer!

Once out in the Indian Ocean I was encouraged by one of the sailors to ask for steering lessons. Officers permission required. The captain or Master as preferred does not steer his ship. The crew do. He's about as required. The 1st mate has the four to eight shift mornings and evenings and is responsible for the day to day running of the vessel and for the loading as well. 2nd mate does twelve to four shifts and usually the navigator The third mate is four til eight and usually not long out of apprenticeship. And the first mate said we're far enough from land to allow for mistakes. In the event it was easy with a large Gyro controlled compass and a nice big wheel.

The next horror came. Crossing the line. If you remember we were three first trip boys likewise the galley boy. The 'ceremony' involves meeting King Neptune. Kissing his feet and being shaved. We boys were having none of it being of a mind that it was another excuse to humiliate us. So rounding up the four of us took some considerable effort. Galley boy being dragged down the mast by his penis. Eventually we were ceremonised. Met Neptune, kissed his feet, got foamed and shaved. Shower and bed. Next day we were presented with nicely drawn certificates to say we had crossed the line (equator) and even felt the bump. I also got a steering certificate for fifty hours steering instruction. Lost them all.

There never seemed to be enough food. Likewise the tea and the milk which was the Condensed variety never seemed to last. The Chief Steward who was responsible for all catering supplies seemed to use the Board of Trade minimum standard as his Bible. In the event, dry stores were issued by the second steward, an odious creature who assured me that the allowance could be increased if I was to do him some 'favours'. If you think I'm doing things for you so the sailors can have a bigger milk ration your very much mistaken.

Being now a day or two out of our first port of call Mombasa the conversation turned to 'bagging off'. Which turned out to visiting the local 'bag shanties' and enjoying the dubious delights of the local women. But your married I said to one. Don't worry lad she'll never know.

We steamed into Mombasa and tied up alongside the jetty and immediately swarmed aboard the local stevedores. Jambo Bwana! A white man in pressed starched khaki drill very much in charge. We unloaded half our cargo over a few days which meant a run ashore. The first stop going with the sailors was the Regal bar, followed by the Britannia bar. Us boys being unused to this found our way to the Missions to Seamen. A large thatched building with full brick gable ends and spaced pillars for the walls. Inside you could get a bar of chocolate and a soft drink. No fridge and the chocolate was soft and sticky. There were chairs arranged facing on gable end where films were shown. The first three rows being armchairs of great age. The films were penny. The armchairs sixpence.

All along the road. A dusty track we were solicited by boys yelling. Hey you want jig-a-jig? My sister, very clean. Take you there now. I think it was a couple of days before

29

we succumbed to both temptation and curiosity and went. Dark, smelly, oil lamps for seeing and ten bob a go. What a lot of fuss about not very much. Mind you when your working on the ship and the chef comes aboard at seven am. you give him a cheer because you know where he's spent the night. We boys had another go a week later and that was a better experience.

We left Mombasa for Dar-es-Salaam in Tanyanika as it was then to discharge the rest of the cargo, Large bay and we were at anchor. Larry suggested a swim. We did, but not realising the outflow from the river delta that Dar'es Salaam occupies pushed us well down the beach on coming out. Never mind the other denizens of the deep that might have enjoyed us. There was nobody to advise us. No one had any responsibility for ships boys. That was the way of things! To comply with Board of Trade regulations, we lowered a lifeboat into the water and rowed round for a bit. Old Paddy taking stroke and saying how it was all done. Good fun! Took most of the morning to accomplish this. Good job we weren't sinking at the time.

Having discharged our cargo we departed for Cape Town to pick up a cargo of bulk (loose) Maize for the UK. Having hosed the ship down and cleaned all the holds from the cement we had to fit shifting boards. These were scaffold like planks that fitted in slots and divided the holds lengthwise. Thus should the ship roll the loose Maize would pile up centre and side rather than on one side. Reduce risk of capsizing. That's when the chippie let me use his Adze for squaring the planks where they'd warped. The chippie was from Newcastle and was looking for a crib partner and decided I was the man. Taught me to play so that we could. At least he wasn't trying to get into my trousers.

CAPE TOWN

All one would expect with Table mountain dominating all. The colour bar was in full force then. Not that we were involved in any of it. Apart from being white. I had a sub as I desperately needed a pair of shoes and we went down town as Larry would have it to get a cheap pair. Had a milk shake and found you got ice cream in them as a matter of course. An evening run found us in the Delmonica; a sort of night club. We never went far and we didn't drink hardly at all. No money. £7.50 a month didn't go far and you could only get a sub against what you had earned not what was to come. Finally loaded and battened down we left for a straight run to Glasgow. The rules were: once you'd discharged a cargo and returned to the U.K. the voyage was complete, and you were paid off. If they liked you you would be invited to return for the next trip. Wherever that might be. If they didn't then you were sacked and given a warrant home. They didn't have to if you agreed to return. Decent companies did anyway. Having entered a man's world I was smoking a bit but rather than face mum's wrath I gave my 200 duty free to Joyce's Ron. Customs came aboard at the 'tail of the bank' Gourock; and to save Larry losing his camera/lighter hobbled around with it my sea boot (wellies). Silly sod. There you go. There was a thick Fog about that time and we were stuck at anchor for a week before moving up the Clyde to discharge. That was the days when there were shipyards all along the banks of the Clyde. we (Britain) had the largest merchant fleet in the world. Still the delay made for a few days extra pay. I and the other two lads were asked to return and were given rail warrants for the home and return journeys. One got a days paid holiday for every month at sea, and for Sundays at sea. You decided when to look for your next job when the money ran out. If you stayed at sea until age 25 one escaped National Service.

PORTSMOUTH

During sea school the family had moved and were living in Denmead flats in Gresham street. I was doing my Naval reserve training and was in R.N. uniform. I remember sitting in the Buffet at Portsmouth and Southsea railway station with mum and were joined by a woman and her daughter about my age. Mum and the woman promptly fell into conversation, while me and the daughter simply looked at each other. What's up with you asked mum. Don't you like girls? Just too shy. Brought up in a boys world. Anyway I was soon off to sea on my first voyage. But dad, ever in hospital died. At least I was home at the time, being between voyages, so we were together as a family. There was a sense of loss: but it hadn't been unexpected. He wasn't a well man. Cremated beyond Porchester now part of the M27. Mum sent me up the Post Office to close his savings account. I was convinced they'd find me out, but the £15 in it was sorely needed.

After the funeral I was to return to Glasgow and mum was keen to return to London. However a woman she met who was on the council persuaded her to look at Leigh Park which was a new development. Phase two just being just started. Mum was impressed and Portsmouth and Leigh park became our home. I was away on my second trip while all this was going on. Sister Joyce and hubby Ron were also persuaded to came and settle there too!

Ron went into nursing, having been a bus conductor, milkman, railway porter had now found his niche in life and he settled in at the Knoll. Suited him down to the ground. Ron's passion after Joyce was cheap paperback cowboy books. cameras, gadgets new, and growing Runner Beans. He'd done his National Service in Palestine and Joyce has a picture of him standing under a camouflage net there. Memory may be a bit off but I've covered all the major points.

BACK to SEA

Back in Glasgow one of the donkeymen. Jock Nichol from Aberdeen took me ashore and we had a drink in a bar opposite the railway station. He allowed me a Double Century, a small bottle of milk stout, and then we went to Kelvin Hall where there was a fun Fair and we had a go on most before back to ship. On another occasion us boys were wandering round Woolworths and one of the girls invited us to a party. We went to make up the numbers. A flat somewhere and we made a date for later post party and went to the Glasgow Empire to see Jerry Colonna. A sort of singer, comedian. Nothing came of anything and we sailed round to Birkenhead to load general cargo. In those days it came piecemeal in Boxes or Crates cartons or sacks and had to be winched aboard with ships Derricks operated by the Stevedores and stowed in the hold using thin planks of old wood called Dunnage to level. They built shelters around the winches against the weather. It was Winter. (December) We seemed to be there for ever before sailing round to Tilbury for the final load. We boys would collect beer bottles from the crew and take them back to the local pubs to collect the tuppences deposit from the bottles. We boys had a couple of runs ashore ourselves, but our money never went far. Larry thought he was on a promise with one girl in a pub and proudly showed me he had the condom on his cock before going ashore. How naive we were. It was at Tilbury and a run ashore and the ferry to Gravesend for the pictures and apres the movie a tattoo parlour for a tattoo. Half a bar. (50p). I felt a real sailor now. We must have sailed eventually and there were some new hands on board, but life changed little for us boys being the bottom of the pile, but we were not unfairly treated.

A week or so into the voyage and I developed a Whicklow on my right thumb. Right under the nail. Bloody painful. The bosun's attempts to find me a left-handed paintbrush never really worked. I'd get up in the night and force matchsticks under the nail to try to relive the pressure. Word must have passed because the chief mate called me into his cabin. Drop your trousers. He gave me a Penicillin injection in the buttocks and no attempts at anything else. Took a chance I suppose, no one was trained to do injections. Worked a treat: the Whicklow was gone in a couple of days. So some time after leaving Tilbury we stopped in Madeira for bunkers. Next stop Cape Town. So we were ashore again for a look round. The second engineer came back in a barrel next morning, He'd been mugged. Then all the ports around the coast. East London. piccy of me somewhere having a swim. Port Elizabeth, Durban. Had a rickshaw ride there. All these places had British administrators working and Union Castle ran passenger vessels to all these places; even up to Mombasa. We did Biera, Lorenco Marques which were in Portuguese hands. Quite a dump both places in my opinion. I was still peggying once every three weeks. Once we'd discharged in Beira we were to Freemantle for grain. Lovely long voyage across the Indian Ocean. I'd got the skipper on the previous voyage to sign my application for King Edward VII college and had my course notes and books. Nories nautical tables and ?? seamanship. Granny had treated me and I'd gone up to Foyles bookshop in Charing Cross to buy them. The learning wasn't too difficult; it was putting up with the jeers of ones peer group. Improving ones position was frowned upon. Well. all those clever apprentices on the first voyage had spurred me on.

FREEMANTLE

Little more than a creek in those days with a few shacks. I sat in a bar with Paddy. He was as old as the hills, or so I thought at seventeen. Nice soft spoken Irishman. We shared a schooner. Funny spoke to a man that had flown out there. Took three days by air. Gentler crowd this time and I avoided the fireman. We were back in Glasgow and not wanting another trip I signed off.

MENDI PALM

having done two voyages as a deck-boy I was now promoted Junior Ordinary Seaman. Pay rise £11 a month. My next ship was the Mendi Palm; one of the Palm line vessels serving the West African coast. She was a bit older than me having been the Leonian when built in '36 The ship was in Rotterdam, and we were sent across from Harwich to the Hook. People had suitcases absolutely covered in stickers of where they had been. This was before Air travel had taken off. We had a couple of nights in a hotel before signing on and getting on board. The ship had Fo'castle accommodation. Two to a cabin. Half the crew were Dutchmen. Brian from Bognor had picked up a hooker somewhere and was going to pass her on to me when finished. The 'lady' in question didn't want this move so he was stuck with her. I was ever so pleased as he had to feed her and the only grub was his! No spare meals. He got her off the boat smartish that night.

The Dutchmen turned out to be nice people. The lad in my cabin was from Liverpool. Can't mind his name. The voyage was down the West Coast of Africa. Every port even rivers. The Gold Coast, Ivory coast, Gambia, Nigeria and French Guinea. We loaded Palm Kernels, Cocoa beans. Sapele trees and whatever else. It was hot and as per regulations we were issued with Solar Toupees. No one of course wore them. There was a mess man to wait tables so I was off the hook there. The officers mess stewards were Black and their cabins were stuffed with old sofas and armchairs; no doubt for the local mud-hut.

Dakar for bunkers and there was a troopship leaving as we went in and every squaddie was hanging over the side watching us. Freetown and a run ashore to try the local beer. There's always one. Enjoying ones pint and he wants to try the local talent and eventually we give in. Mind you there were some comely young girls at ten bob a go! You may think I'm being gross but that was the way of it. There were no considered moral issues. We were callow youth! At Cotonou we were invited by the local administrators for drinky poos. They sent a rail car for us with a local driver. We spent the evening playing snooker and having black staff wait upon us. All very colonial. For the return the driver wanted 'dash' which we never had or refused to pay. So he took his railcar away and we had to walk back through the Jungle.

At Freetown we took on local Kroo boys to do the Stevedore work as we travelled the coast. There was a huge steam boiler on the foredeck where they cooked their food. A the chippie built a wood and sacking contraption over the stern where they could 'do their business'. Had a couple of nears misses when painting the ship aft. It's called being shit upon from a great height. Not a pretty sight either. One stop was Appapa across the river from Lagos. The ferry across was a penny but they routinely charged us sixpence.

Not that there was much one wanted to buy. It was about the French Guinea that I developed severe itching in the groin. Inspection showed I had contracted Pubic Lice, or 'Crabs' as colloquially known. Saw the chief steward and got some powder. One of the Dutchmen followed suit a day later. Liberally dusting his arse and wedding tackle in full view of the bridge. Others followed with the exception of my cabin mate, So he was the obvious carrier. I threw him out the cabin and the crew rallied round and he was dosed up against his will. Bugger was ashore every night, dipping his wick. Barely had a stitch of clothing left. He'd bartered it all. The tailor man who came aboard in Liverpool was more than happy to take him away for new clothing so he could leave the ship. I never wanted to do another trip on that old scow, or see the West coast of Africa again. So I paid off and went home. On route to London on the Red Rose Express an apprentice I was travelling with suggested we go the buffet car for dinner. Can't I say. I don't know which knife and fork to use. He showed me.

While away the family had moved to Winterslow Drive in Leigh Park. A great change for the better from Gresham Street. I needed to be shown where we lived. Mum and Mike met me. I can't for the life of me remember how we did it. Never mind mobiles, we never even had a phone. We're walking up Dunsbury Way and mother's saying we'll have a party to introduce you to the local girls. Michael can organise them. I don't know any girls say Mike. Oh Hello Betty who was riding her bike up Dunsbury Way. Little did I know that I had just met my future wife. We had the party, no booze. Well I invited Pammy Bradshaw from a few doors up to the movies. No good you going out with her said mum: she belongs to Charlie Duhamel in spite of her mother's wishes. She did! They married and got a flat nearby. So I turned my attention to Betty as being the only alternative and started taking her out. There was a bevy of girls in the local paper shop in Botley Drive but I was too shy to ask one out off the bat. We did the movies. Or, a bus to Pompey and a walk down the Commercial Road window shopping and up the other side, and then on to Nan Tirrells. Say hello to her and uncle George. Bus back. Wonderfully exciting stuff, but money was short. Must have been about Easter because I remember buying her an Easter Egg. Jim Logie feeling that he at last had a man in the place he could discuss that merits of Portsmouth F.C. must have been more than disappointed with my reply. No likee football. Then of course it was back to sea to earn some money.

THE MARSDALE (Volta River)

I'd seen this old scow down the west coast what a heap of junk. Funny it was as old as me. I'd been to the Pool with Brian from Bognor who'd been on the Mendi with me and wanted to sail with me again. We were sent to look at a tramp doing Persian Gulf and Aussie: seven months. Brian was courting and didn't want to go away that long. Life changing moment. Tell Brian, tough I fancy it. Or go with him? And we found ourselves on the Marsdale, even though I didn't want to do the west coast again I went along with him.

The ship was in Hamburg, so we never got a chance to look at it. We did a couple of three days in a hotel.

Taxied to ship for days work. I was in with a French Canadian. Fat, odious man. Omen. The crew were a mixed bunch. Jocks, scousers, Kiwis, Frenchie. Shitbag. (had a huge gut). Everybody hated everybody. The ship was bad enough. Ex Merchant cruiser so they said. Skipper had been on it since birth. (it's).

First port of call was Bathurst in Gambia where the Bosun walked off it. And after that as they say it was all downhill. The skipper liked to have bells rung like in the old navy. A bell every half hour augmented till eight at four hours. He said to me in the Atlantic. Your not steering this ship sonny, your sculling it! Well your streerings clapped out. Took them half a day to fix it. Spent Christmas Day in Takoradi harbour, 25 degrees, no wind. Full Xmas dinner, bored witless I went ashore in a surf boat that we'd had as deck cargo to buy some beer for the crew. At the harbour gate on return the coppers wanted 'dash' (a kickback). Common in Nigeria. I refused and was slung in the nick. Fortunately they let me out after a couple of hours and I was able to return to the ship where there were tales of robbery. To whit; one surf boat. What we were going to do with a damn great wooden boat, heaven above knows.

Finally all that finished and the coastal ports and rivers and we sailed across to Vittorio in Brazil for Iron Ore. Iron Pyrites. The usual run ashore. There were umpteen Cruzerios to the pound. In a bar as usual. (what else to do?) the girls wore a large key around their necks signalling availability. The Celanese cook, built like a rail, said to me. You English do it all wrong. Too much beer before have jig-a-jig one time. I have girl, drink Coke and have another girl. Well each to his own. Cecilia was a very nice one. This cargo was for Rotterdam Madeira for bunkers, where I picked up a Monkey. I came through Harwich where customs had a 'magic eye' and woe betide anyone smuggling. I had the monkey in my jacket looking out. Anything to declare? No! I actually forgotten the monkey. And we were through. At Waterloo I asked a mate to hold it for me while I went the loo. When I got back it had shit all down his nice suit. No: I simply took the monkey and walked away. Mum spotted it the moment I arrived at Winterslow. Your not bringing that in here, away with you. In the event it lived on the sideboard with it's monkey manners until we persuaded the Blue Cross to take it. Finished up in Pompey zoo. Had a stiff middle finger, so I recognised it. Glad to be rid of it anyway.

EDH

Efficient Deck Hand. Up to now if you'd served long enough the 'pool' could rate you up to Senior ordinary seaman. The next step was a two week training course at the training ship in the West India Docks. Bigger stuff. I stayed at the Stack of Bricks which was a hostel of sorts. 4/- (20p) got you a bed in a four foot walled cubicle with three others. 10/- (50) got you a room, which I elected for. The course was about the finer points of seamanship and not difficult and we came away with our rating. So, down to the pool for another job. Need a short trip, I'm courting. They sent me to Dagenham docks and the Sithonia. A fast built vessel to help replace wartime losses.

SITHONIA

40

The vessel was discharging bulk cane sugar at the Tate and Lyle plant at Dagenham. Mini bulldozers pushing it into heaps for the grabs to handle. It wasn't long before we'd unloaded and were sailing for Cuba for more. Young crowd no Brian from Bognor and we all got along famously. Bullshitting Banyard from Ipswich; had an endless fund of stories. My Greek mate who's name escapes me became firm friends. The only fly in the ointment was a lad on his first trip as EDH and he wanted to 'challenge' me over every task we did. I don't like competition for no particular reason. The ship needed cleaning and the more we hosed the 'stickier' it became.. We got there in the end. At days end one had to pump up the water by hand, and while one did so some bugger would be in there taking a shower. All taken in good part. We arrived in Santiago De Cuba in about ten days and began loading sugar. Sacks were hoisted aboard and placed on a grid leading to a funnel: split the sacks and the sugar runs down to an electric driven belt with a man directing the sugar around the hold, including the corners.

There was a revolution going on. Castro against Batista for the country. (we all know who won that contest). A run ashore found us in the American bar. Two dollars (US) got one a bottle of Rum, tray of ice, tray of Limes, five cokes and a girl on all your laps. Not bad. The girls topped up the drinks. Elvis Presley's Blue Suede Shoes on the jukebox: magic! I remember buying a St Christopher and vaguely returning to the ship and waking about two am. with the biggest hangover ever. Next run was dependent on the gate guard saying O.K. no revolution tonight. That's also where I discovered Anisette. Couldn't believe how it changed colour. Four of us got a bus into town one weekend, do the tourist bit. The driver hanging out the window cheering the local talent or merely haloing the shopkeepers. About a week and we were on our way back. I bought Betty a Cuban bracelet made of painted wooden disks. I did make a point of buying her bracelets but never saw them on her. No, no nookie this time. I had a word with Stella who had a look standing in the bar, to see if I was clean! But for some reason we never did owt about it. On arrival back at London Docks, we were boarded by customs. To be expected and taxi drivers coming aboard as we entered the lock gates. They were touting for business straight away. Get a cabful lined up. Scoff someone's breakfast and hang about until pay-off. We cleaned ourselves up and with a loan from the taxi driver it was down the pub. Getting back in time to sign off. Then away. Customs release forms were handed to the driver who passed them over to the dockyard policeman along with half a crown from each of us. (to ensure swift passage). thence to ones railway station and home. So back to Leigh Park and courtship. Pictures, walk, bike ride. Betty was quite content with that. Did try the pub once but it wasn't a success. No drinks for women in those days. Gin and Orange or Port and Lemon. Babycham didn't exist.

The money ran out and I said to Betty I'll get another short trip. Took the chance to see my Greek mate. His parents had a cafe in Frith street, Soho. So we tried the clubs. Ten bob membership and secrete a half of scotch so you only bought one drink. The 'girls' tended to leave us alone. No chance to make a shilling there. They could probably pick a 'mark' from experience and me and the Greek were hardly going to make them any money.

STS VELLETIA

SHELL TANKER s.t.s. "VELLETIA" 28,106 D.W. TONS

I said to the chap in the pool, I need a short trip. Got a King boat he say. No ta. Twelve months far east. How about a James boat? No ta. Two years far east. I was beginning to know ships and shipping. Well he say go round to Joe Shell in the Minories. They recruit direct. So round I go. Got a V boat he say or a Cap boat. Shell surprisingly named their vessels after the Latin names of shells. The initial giving you the tonnage. Thus a cap boat: Capriata was eighteen thousand tons and the V Velletia, Volvatella, twenty-eight thousand tons. Simple. I only want a short trip I say. Well it's Mena Al a Madhi to load and Lands End for orders. So you have a chance of returning every thirty days. I opted for the V boat and was given a sub and told to return in a few days as the ship was in Hamburg. Travel by rail and ferry. This was my first Tanker and I was surprised to find one got one's own cabin. Mind you the ship was big enough. 810ft length and 56 wide. Fairly young crowd. We had a weekend for sightseeing and a trip down the Riperbhan to see scantily clad young girls putting on a floor show. Never the likes in England. After the delights of Hamburg we found ourselves anchored off Cowes I.o.W. along with the Volvatella at 29,000 tons which immediately became the 'big ship'. Compared to us at 28,000. We used to meet at runs ashore in Cowes. There was a world glut of oil and we were waiting for a decision. I asked the chief mate if I could pop home for the weekend. Which he agreed to. Two other lads did likewise but never returned.

The Velletia was a steam turbine vessel capable of eighteen knots. The decision was to shut down one boiler and reduce her speed to twelve knots. Easing the oil glut as it were. I was given the job of chipping the paint off a Samson Post and Smudger Smith the other one. Smudger came from Middlesboro and built like Clint Walker. He said he'd like a gang of kids and be able to line them up and dish out the dosh for the pictures. I wonder if he ever did? Nice bloke. Back to Samson Posts. The noise of the paint chipping annoyed the skipper especially in the pm. as it spoiled his kip. Not my fault, but I got the flak. Normally the bosun would sort out the work at his store dishing out the paint or Suji and when you ran out you went and got some more. Joe Shell had a store man. I spent more time on that ship looking for the bloody store man, because his store was always locked. Who was to Nick it? There was only us on board. Eventually I went up to the mates cabin, where he was taking a shower and said if I can't get any stores I'm not doing any more work. Of course the shit hit the fan and I was in the draft. The bosun said you should have come to me. Nobody could see it from my point of view.

I was on the 12-4 shift with Ernie, who was forever wandering into my cabin and offering me his cock to play with. We had an Irishman,a young lad who having one over the eight in Hamburg went round the deck dumping things like life rings, rope, over the side. Caused a general charge on all of us on deck. The first task on any Tanker after discharge is 'tank cleaning'. A large heavy garden type sprinkler is lowered into a tank and hot sea water sprays about. The device is lowered three times and then moved to the next tank. Twenty-seven in all and the work is continuous. Overtime for all. Off to Kuwait via the Suez Canal. Must have taken about two weeks. Once there you can have the oil as fast as you want it. We loaded at seven thousand tons and hour. Which gave us time to walk down the jetty and have a free fanta in the cool canteen before returning to sail. Six and a half hours in port!. So! Lands End here we come. Didn't even get close. La Spezia Italy.

The ship had a cinema on board, being a screen slung between two Samson posts. One would take a chair from one's cabin and a couple of Mars bars. From the bond one could buy fags, booze and sweets. I think this might have been a private enterprise by the captain. Most skippers restricted the issue of beer to twice a week and amount to prevent drunkenness. The chief thief as he was known. (chief steward) said to me and Ernie. 'Buy' two hundred fags and I'll let you have a dozen beers instead. So twice a week we'd have a case of beer. Sailing up the Persian Gulf it was hot, hot, hot. There was a tap on the bulkhead that ran through the fridge. We drank so much of this 'ice water' that we all had little beer bellies. There was also a swimming pool. A large square canvas bag with wooden sides and steel bracers. Most welcome. Having enjoyed it in the Red Sea plunging in the Mediterranean came as a shock. Good handover cure!

So to repeat. Back to Mina and back to Italy and back to Mena and load for Portland Maine. About thirty days travel. My Navigation was coming along and I charted the course from Gibraltar to Portland and was right. Yippee! We got to Portland, Maine about Xmas or New Year. Perry Como was doing Magic Moments. Never mind the oil we had a marathon load of dry stores to load and I managed to filch a jar of Maxwell House coffee, which lasted me for ages.

I'm sitting in a cafe/bar. Coffee. You have to be twenty-one drink in the US of A. There's a group of girls at a table along and one is marrying a Greek. Her friend was saying that Greeks are into Buggery; so be prepared. The reply was: as long as it's me he's buggering. I don't care where he puts it. Ernie was still wandering into my cabin hoping I'd play with his cock.. From the cafe we went to a tailors and I bought a couple of pairs of Levis Jeans and a radio. Had to have a short waveband as there was very little to listen to. Ernie nagging me I eventually gave in and swapped the radio for a hand tailored overcoat. Nice coat.

From Portland we were down to New York. Our next port of call being Curacao in the Dutch West Indies and because of the low rainfall and the need for vast amounts of water for industrial use; one had to arrive full of the stuff; even if they threw it away. N.Y. Pick up a pilot and sail up the Hudson river until it was fresh water and load. I'm on the wheel and the pilot says to the captain. How high is the mast? 112ft above the waterline. Well best you get some water in her the next bridge is only 110ft. Somewhere just past Sing-Sing we took on water and sailed for Punta Cardon. Curacao.

Just a refinery and we are soon loaded and on our way to Rotterdam. We are getting long voyage syndrome now. At Rotterdam we were just about out of victuals and after an apology for a breakfast four of us went ashore and had a nice plate of Ham and Eggs and then did the tourist bit. Me, Mick the Irishman, a Scotsman and of course Ernie. I got Betty a nice compact. (never saw her use it). We had our photo taken in some bar and later that day borrowed someone's bicycle from another bar and there's this drunk cycling around Rotterdam trying to avoid the tramlines and the traffic to collect our photo's. I managed it and had the one of us in the bar on our 'fine' notification stuck up in my cabin with 'the clique' as a caption. The fine was one days loss of pay and one days loss of earnings. Doubling for the next offence. Spent the next day loading dry stores and beer. Got myself a nice set of glasses to take home eventually. Orangeboom. We had a new chief mate join and the bosun left the ship at once. He and the new chief had issues in the past. From Rotterdam we did the whole round trip again, Mena, Portland, Curacao, Rotterdam. Perry Como was still singing Magic Moments. From Rotterdam second time we did Mena and Le Harve. I am seriously considering swimming the channel for home. So much for. Lands End for orders. We did Le Harve twice and then Newcastle for refit and discharge. Eleven months and ten days. How this documents survived all these years I can't imagine. All of the photos I took while at sea were lost.

I paid off with £107. 5d but of my allotment home to mum of £231 was saved and most of it returned to me. Bless her

I was going to need it. Not that I was aware of it then.

The first thing I did was to buy myself an H.Samuel Everite watch. They were advertised on Radio Luxumberg and this was for me. It kept very good time but would stop from time to time and it was a £1 each time to have it repaired. Forced to do it myself once being back at sea. One discovered a wrist hair had worked it's way in and trapped the hair spring. I turned it round and wore it on the underside of my wrist. No problems after that.

ACCOUNT OF WAGES
(Sec. 133, M.S.A. 1894)

Keep this Form as a Record of
Your Nat. Insurance and Income Tax Deductions

NAME OF SEAMAN

Dis. "A" No.

Name of Ship and Official Number	Class	Section	Income Tax Code	Rating	Ref. No. in Agreement

U.
G.S.
C.S.
List

A or B

Nat. Insurance No.
Contributions commence
Monthly

(DATE)

Date Wages Began	Date Wages Ceased	Total Period of Employment		Allotment Note given for		
		Months	Days	Amount	Date 1st Payment	Interval

EARNINGS

Wages... months @ £ ... per month
days @ £ ... per day
Increase in Wages (Promotions, etc.)
From... to... @ £... per mth. ... mths. ... days
From... to... @ £... per mth. ... mths. ... days

Overtime ... hours @ ... per hour
... hours @ ... per hour

Leave and Subsistence brought fwd. ... days
Voyage Leave ... days
Sundays at Sea ...
Total ...
Leave taken ...
Balance due ... days @ £ ... per day
Subsistence ... days @ £ ... per day

Delete as necessary { Carried forward to next voyage
{ Paid—to be shown in Earnings Column

Total Earnings

Less Reduction by £ ... p.m. ... mths. ... days

Earnings
Deductions
Final Balance

DEDUCTIONS

Advance on Joining
Allotments
Fines
Forfeitures
Pension Fund ... No.
Income Tax ... Months at
Union Contributions:
... weeks at ...
Insurance (Voyage)
... weeks at ...
Wireless Messages
Postages
Tobacco
Wines
Stores
Canteen
Cash

Total Deductions

ADJUSTMENTS

Add

Deduct

£

National Insurance paid to date wages ceased.
*National Insurance paid on leave to
*This line to be deleted if it does not apply.

Signature of Master

SEE OVER   Nº 33

A PAYING OFF SLIP

So with nothing much better to do Betty and I fell to
courting again. The movies, Commercial Road figuring
largely in all this. Ma and Pa Logie never moved outside
the door apart from one night, and that's when I proposed.
Proposed?. I never even knew the woman. So, off to H.
Samuels in Pompey and buy an engagement ring. Once the

manager realised I was spending a months money he elbowed the assistant aside and served me himself. The ring cost me £33. Having decided then that we were going to marry I asked her father's hand in marriage. Jim Logie said he was more than pleased, but we'd have to wait until he'd saved some money. Sod that I say. I'll pay for it!

Didn't Ma Logie enjoy putting her hand out for the cash and pushing off with the daughters in tow for a shopping spree. I jibbed when asked for money to buy the bridesmaids a gift. I'd bought them dress each: what more? Pay up Parker. My mother was well enough pleased as she harboured a thought that I might be queer or at least a bit bent and was in a hurry to see it happen. I don't think I loved Betty. More that I was in love with love. St Francis, Leigh Park for the nuptials and after at the pub at the junction of Stockheath road and the Petersfield road. Had a family room. Now called the Heron.

Come the Honeymoon I was skint just about and at mum's suggestion we stayed with a friend of hers in Balham. Trips to the city were the order of the day. Trafalgar Square. Take your picture Only ten bob. Be ready Thursday. Sucker lost that ten bob. Thief. The highlight was a trip to The Brevet Flying Club Mayfair organised by uncle Con. and a taxi ride to see the ladies of the night in Piccadilly. Hot stuff!

Mum had moved to Botley Drive and had her parents living with her, so there was no room for Bet and I. Consequently we moved in with Bet's mum and dad. They moved out of their room and I redecorated it as per instructions.
And Betty and I moved in there. Not the best arrangement but until Portsmouth Council came through on our application for a council house; we were stuck with each other. Wether it was having Harry Tyler on the council married to Betty's aunt. Eileen. Or the fact they were building Leigh Park like mad: Bet and I got one at 4

Rockbourne Close and moved in. Lovely. We had a double bed that Gran had bought, and Lebus furniture from Mennards in Havant. Stair carpet, but no carpets upstairs. The headboard was a strip of Fablon. Betty's friends would call round for a cheap night out: or in. Gray and Les. Clive and Rose Mr and Mrs Duhamel (Charlie and Pammy Bradshaw).

I took a job with British Rail on the Ferries from the harbour to the Isle of Wight where I met Jake Witcher. He was a ships engineer, and I needed him! Joyce s Ron had given me his motor bike and sidecar. He'd invested in a scooter and being impressed by my mechanical knowledge. It was an Aerial Red Hunter 500cc twin ports and absolutely clapped out. Any problems I couldn't manage and I went to Jake. It only had a lump of Sorbo rubber as a pillion and would never start if Betty was there. She had to hide round a corner before the bloody thing would fire up. True! And it leaked oil from the rocker covers and would smoke as it burned off from the cooling fins. Eventually sold it to a bloke with the 350 Aerial for spares. £10. He never got a thing off it he could use.

The ferry. There was an American lad working there whom had left home after a row with mum and dad. But good fun. People having problems boarding were assisted. We even carried a man and his wheelchair aboard. Tips for handling luggage were passed to the purser who divided them up at weeks end. Not everyone was on luggage detail. Occasionally we'd do a trip to Southampton to see the liners. I'm on the wheel and the mate's doing a commentary over the Tannoy. The Purple ship is. Psst! Union Castle's colours are Magenta and they call at. A much better commentary after that with my coaching The season came to an end. The American got his call-up papers and went home to mum and dad: tout suite. And Mother came round and said I've got you a job. It's a deep sea tug. The Prosperous, Royal Fleet Auxillary, lying on the North Wall,

Pompey dockyard.

Basically it was a day job I'd cycle down from Leigh Park and we'd do things on the ship. Put to sea from time to time and play convoys with the navy. Racked up in Weymouth and on a run ashore went round to the Boot Hotel here A man that had joined the Velletia as a late late replacement lived. He was there and he joined the crew of the Prosperous. They christened him 'the Nut'. He was a bit off.

We then get a commission to tow an inshore Minesweeper to Aden. Cheaper than sailing it there I suppose. I'm on the wheel somewhere off the bottom end of Spain and the skipper with his Goatee and looking every inch an old sea dog; says to me. I've seen more ships on the left, so Gibraltar must be over that way. So go over that way a bit. Doesn't give you much faith in the navigator. We found Gibralter and I was quite taken with how clean and tidy everything was. I bought a 400 day clock there. Next stop was Malta to refuel. It was there or Cyprus. Couldn't get any at Suez. Because of the recent invasion of Egypt we were PNG.

A drink in Malta, do a pee in the bucket behind the curtain. Avoid Screech as the local vino was called at 2/- a bottle. Then off to Suez and transit through the canal. We 'strapped' the minesweeper alongside us for the trip through..When at sea she (the Tug) was a hungry feeder as the chief thief was buying a car on the amount he would make this trip. He was quite open about it. I lost half a stone without trying. They took the Minesweeper off us at Aden and berthed it with the intention of berthing us alongside. The pilot is gingerly approaching this minesweeper when the skipper takes over. More speed: a tug can stop on a sixpence. Except he'd forgotten that we were touch and go on fuel and the prop was half out of the water. We were within an ace of wrecking the ship we'd brought so far. The run ashore in Aden, Crater, later to star in Major Mike Hoares career. Not much, shops and dirt. From Aden we got a call to go and standby a Maersk tanker that had been in a collision. We played escort up the Red Sea Then got a call to find a warship and basically exchanged signals with her. We carried a Naval Trained Signalman. He was a worshipper of Aliester Crowley. Skippers sporting a new pipe and I asked the 'old goat'. (our eldest crew member). Don't you have break a pipe in? Nah he say, he bought it second hand. Got it off a Doctor. Bunkering again in Malta we returned to our spot on the North Wall in Pompey. Customs came aboard and we got chits for the dockyard coppers. Just as well as the copper on the gate at the time was all for confiscating my 'perfumed spirits'. no, he never got his hands on it. So bus home to Betty. Seems she had got bored living on her own and gone back to live with mum. Only trouble was she never cleared out the larder and the place stunk and the flies were enormous. And no, she hadn't bothered to go to Havant and pay Mennards their pound a week for the furniture. An on going fault with her! Paying the tally man. She's cost me a months wages to clear her tally at 11 Iping.

After that run the ship was due a refit. We took the lifeboats off her (two). Used the motorised one to tow the other across to the boat yard. By the time we reached it the pulling boat had all but sunk and the motor boat sunk a week later.

I got sick, Flu or something and got the sack from the tug being unavailable for work. Done me a favour really.
Betty told me she was pregnant. Oh! So it does work like that. So I took a job in Southern Garages on the Cosham road selling petrol. Petrol was 4/6 a gallon (23p) for premium shell and 4/1 for Power. Oil was kept in bottles but if you could persuade a motorist to try Shell Detergent oil which came in tins and carried a nice premium. We staff had a share of the profits from Shell A few bob but welcome. Old Arthur and me on the pumps. A bloke in the

oil bay doing the servicing. Mr Merrick the foreman. A boss and a couple in the workshop. Then bombshell!

I got a brown envelope telling me to report to The White Knights building at Reading? My call-up papers. I was still eligible for National Service. Someone was keeping an eye on me. So I was off to the pool in Southampton pretty quick for a job.

CAMITO

This was a passenger cargo vessel belonging to Elders and Fyffes the Banana people. I'd been to the 'pool' in Southampton and was told that as I had been away for so long I must go before a committee to explain myself. They said I could return if I took a pier head jump on the Camito. Literally board as she was leaving harbour. I found out why she couldn't recruit. Had a bad reputation. I was told four to eight lookout. No tricks on the wheel and no hours break during the shift. (not how it should work).

Basically being a Banana boat and fairly fast we only had ten days to clean holds for the new cargo. The four to eight lookout-me also had to wash the teakwork rails down with fresh water in the mornings, One of the stewards came up to me and said the last bloke would go down his cabin and masturbate. I could do it for you. We ignored that. The ship being a passenger vessel had one enormous advantage for us young lads. It fed magnificently. Cooked breakfast, toast at tea break, three course lunch, high tea and dinner at eight. Boy! That was me until first stop Barbados, then on to Trinidad and thence to Jamaica. We had the English test team on board and they would practise on deck. A Kingston we anchored off and there were liberty boats for a run ashore. They never used to but the crews kicked up over it. I'd gone ashore with Geoff from my cabin to try the local Red Stripe beer. We got separated and I'm on my own in the gents when I feel another hand doing the business for me. What a big man she say. Just what I am looking for. So it was round to her place. At least it wasn't a mud hut. From Kingston it was round to Montego bay to begin loading. There was a bar there and sitting around having a drink with five or six girls sitting with us when 'Debbie' came in. Debbie was one of the stewards and in the vernacular of the day. Fruit. (today gay!). All the girls rushed over to 'her'. full of animation. Later quite a bit later 'Debbie' was going back to the ship and being tired or whatever I said I'll come with you. Well the looks of scorn and derision I got from the girls. I never did. By reputation Debbie was fussy and wouldn't perform as usual for queers. I really did return to my cabin. I'd had enough Red Stripe and Appleton's Estate for anyone.

Once we had returned and were a day out from Avonmouth we were invited to the bosun's cabin and offered a Rum and a 'will you come back next trip'? It was guaranteed a short trip so I said OK if as a day worker. No more four hour lookouts. Plenty of overtime. They were the gang cleaning holds. The bosun had been on the ship yonks and knew to the second how long a task should take. So if he had you painting a lifeboat. The moment you'd finished he was there. No time for a fag and then go look for him. People didn't like this, so the ship couldn't recruit. The second trip was cleaning and preparing the holds for the Bananas and the amount of Banana spiders that had survived not only the insecticide but the refrigerated crossing. Don't let the bosun's mate know your scared of them or he'll throw them at you. Yewk! I hated them.

Jamaica this time was less exciting thank goodness and Geoff wasn't happy that his 'girl' was waiting for him on the dock. He wanted a change. Bananas are cut as the ship arrives, trained down to the docks. One bunch to a man. Dipped in insecticide, wrapped in Polythene and a tally collected as they are brought aboard and stowed. On leaving the vessel, one was allowed a bunch to take home. Good eh? The second return voyage was a bugger as we appeared to be following the same course and speed as a low depression and it rained nearly all the way back. A sailors life for me. I complained at breakfast of soft searching hands in the night. Couple of the other lads likewise. No doubt one of the queers, but he'd got short shrift. Glass of Rum with the bosun but no more ta. And home to Betty and the baby. Well the bump.

It was high Summer as they always seemed to be in those days. Betty could rest a cup of tea on it. And the maternity dresses were at full stretch. A woman was expected to 'hide' her condition. Right Ma she'll be having it in Hospital. No she'll have it at home. I lost that argument. Come the day; Betty went into labour early evening in that small room downstairs. Midwife was called and I went round to get my mum. Even though there was no love lost between her and Dink. The labour dragged on. Gas and air and entreaties didn't help. Endless cups of tea were made and eventually in the early hours the midwife called the doctor. Dopey Dilnot as he was referred to. He called the hospital and the flying squad came out. Forceps delivery about 5 am. Betty had Toxaemia and eclamsia. Overlooked or not known due to me having A-Neg blood. Before rushing both mum and baby off to St Mary's the doc said no more babies for at least three years. Mum said to me Come on we'll walk round to Joyce's and let her know you have a daughter.

I went back to working locally. Got a job as a general labourer on a site in Horndean. He was building a dozen or so houses in Love Lane. I still had the motor-bike and used that for travel. The chippy would pillion to save petrol, until a mishap in Leigh Park where an inner tube I'd stuffed carelessly under the saddle made it's way between the drive chain, locking the back wheel and sending us across the road. No traffic happily. We used his car after that. The job was OK but the boss was not getting his money and the banks were being awkward and we went on short money. Winter was coming and yearning for the warmer climes I decided to go back to sea.

The 'pool' offered me the Thornaby; a Ropner boat lying at Weymouth. A tanker built 1955 and only 12000 odd tons . I joined her and went along to the Boot Hotel where the 'nut's' dad kept the pub. We then sailed for Thameshaven to load.

M.V. THORNABY

She was to be my last vessel but I was unaware of that at the time. So Thameshaven to load for Sweden. A new apprentice joined us there and his father came down to see the chief mate and ensure he looked after his boy! He was so promised. We sailed from there to Sanjeford in Sweden just inside the Arctic Circle' Normal routine was a 7a.m.

start, but as it was so bloody cold they left us 'til 8. As we travelled the Kiel Canal all the houses had lit Christmas trees out and a real Christmas card scene it all looked.

The people of Sanjeford gave us a small gift each. I got a string vest. We went to a local dance where they served tea. The pubs only opened between 5&6 and the stuff was far too expensive. I did have the grace to get a postcard and send it to the building site. The second cook and baker had the dirtiest pair of underpants imaginable. They sacked him in Newcastle when we returned there after Sweden. Technically I could have left the ship there having completed a voyage, discharged a cargo and returned to UK. Nobody did. Apart from the cook. We tied up in the river Tyne near the original bridge I was aft with the after crowd mooring the vessel with the second mate in charge. We were instructed to use the Insurance Cable. Huge Bloody thing as thick as your arm. Why? we were in a river. It was on a cable drum on the top deck and due to it's weight ran away with us. A bloke run up the ladder to apply the brake; someone had left the handle in and it flew off and smashed him in the face. He never came back. Had to get a diver to retrieve the cable.

So from Newcastle to Japan. And the ships routine reverted to 7a.m. start. I was on watch with another Ernie and the new apprentice. Eight 'til Noon and eight till midnight. No swimming pool on this one or movies. The 'new' apprentice who'd relieved me complained that when he called to wake the chief mate; he'd whip back the bedding and say to the lad. Have a play with this. What to do? Spit on it I say. I can't he say, lose my indentures. We were doing sheet change and I said to the mate. You remind me of a film star. Whom? He ask preening. Margaret Rutherford. Later when we were working on deck he called me round to my cabin and before you could say knife; he'd closed the porthole, had my shorts up and my cock in his mouth. Crumbs, the chief officer! He would come up when

57

I was on lookout in the dark and drag me to the windlass for cover so he could repeat the exercise. Madness for a man in his position. And so much for my advice. Spit on it!

KAWASAKI JAPAN 1960

The local blurb. Yokasuka where over a thousand prostitutes roam the streets. That was without those in bars and clubs, The first pub ashore and it was early afternoon but the owner insisted on getting his girls out of bed in spite of our assurances that we were moving on. Me and three others took a taxi to Yokohama. Got settled in a local bar. Girls all round. I wanted to buy a Teddy Bear for my Jackie and trying to explain it to the bar girls. They took me to the zoo, then the pier for some reason. Back to pub, more sign language and suddenly one of the girls took me round the corner to a shop full of Teddy Bears, all shapes and sizes. There wasn't enough money left to discover whether it was true that Japanese girls have their fanny going crossways. So taxi back to the ship. The next evening, nobody had enough money for a run ashore, so we all gathered in one blokes cabin to compare notes. Later two of the lads got some rope and unravelled it to make a long wig of sorts and with their trophy bra and knickers (nothing else) went round the other cabins displaying their allure. Come later when the bloke whose cabin it was wanted to go to bed and the rest of us were still enjoying the night. I said, go and sleep in my cabin and I'll sleep in yours. No problem until the morn when he returned to dress for work and I'm still in bed and the Bosun's there to call us for work: and saw what he saw and based on the previous nights performance immediately jumped to the wrong conclusion. That went round the ship like wildfire. Took days to live down.

On leaving Japan the apprentice that I was on shift with me and us both being eternally hungry decided to break in to the galley for a midnight feast. There was a stable door between the crew mess and the galley and with a bit of judicious work with a bit of thin line and a loop managed to snag the bolt and we were in. It was about 1a.m. a couple of fried egg sarnies later and how to relock the door? The Galley's porthole was open next to it's steel stable door and the key was in the lock. Open door pass through, close door, reach through porthole and replace key. We used that method ever after. We were on deck and the apprentice called me to look at Mount Fujiama which had appeared through the clouds but I missed it. They say if you see Fujiama you will return to Japan, but I never did.

Next stop Bombay. We'd hardly anchored before the sellers were aboard. Do your corns Sahib? I don't have corns. An ancient man in a turban insisted on telling me my fortune. He read my forehead and said these words.

Your life is divided roughly roughly into three parts,
1st part not very special. second part much the same,
third part best of all. You will get sick three times.
you will never have any money but you'll never broke
you will know much love.

Virtually verbatim to what the Egyptian said four years before in the canal when he read my palm.

For the run ashore we went to a missions to seamen but there was little on. Some wonderful Ivory carvings, but out of my reach. So four of us took a taxi tour of Bombay from the Pukka Sahib's quarters along the Queens necklace they call the corniche round the bay: then further in to Bombay. At nineteen years of age I thought I had seen a bit of the world but I'd never seen such poverty. I thought the West coast Africans were pretty short of things, but Bombay? People living in the streets, lying in rags. Then to the cages. An area like the red light district where rows of tenements with cages facing the street instead of doors and up to five girls working in each one. Driver say one Rupee for girl and ten for doctor after. He then took us out of there to a bar I thought. Upstairs and sit. No bar, we're in a brothel I said to my mate. We got a beer and the apprentice; he of the galley raids, built like a Greek god even with the fair curls and the physique to match. Said to me, I fancy a woman but if I get the 'clap' I'll lose my indentures. Well I say, see the Mama and she'll supply. Suitably equipped he went out with this willow of a girl in a sari and she returned ten fifteen minutes later, not a hair out of place. He staggered in looking like he'd gone fifteen rounds with Mike Tyson, but well satisfied. No one else indulged and we returned to the ship. Cost about 5 Rupees; not each but the whole trip.

From Bombay we had a run up the coast small place and a run ashore gave us a game of football against the local team on their earthen ground. Thence again to Kuwait for a load of crude and the voyage home paying off at Thames Haven. As a bit of horseplay the lads wrestled me to the ground and put a bloody great love bite on my neck. Once home Betty never even mentioned it. I was still working on and off at this second mates ticket but life kept getting in the way. Should have been a second mate by now

THE ROYAL AIR FORCE
Per Ardua Ad Astra

1960 and another great Summer. What to do now? I'd been feeling like I needed a bit of a change. Being newly married with a child I didn't want to keep going to sea. Betty would move back to her mum's place, the bills wouldn't get paid and no doubt the pantry would be left as is. I was round Mum's in Botley Drive. She'd moved again, when brother Mike came in in his new uniform. He'd joined the RAF. That's an idea I'll join the forces. Tried the Naval recruiting office. Yes, no problem they say: seaman gunner, nine year engagement. I don't want to be a seaman gunner I want to be an artificer. (electrical/mechanical technician). No lad. Seaman gunner, prime material. Stuff you I thought and went round to the Army. Don't ask me why. Real old dad's army type of a duffer in there didn't seem to have a clue what to offer me. Gave me a couple of leaflets in the end.

I finally racked up with the RAF in Lake Road. The Warrant Officer there asked me some questions and asked if I'd mind doing a couple of tests which I was quite happy to do. Once finished and marked (they were multiple choice answers). He say to me I can offer you a radar mechanics course: your not quite ready for a fitters course. Three year engagement. I was getting used to this lark now and the opportunity to learn a trade was a big incentive, So I signed on the dotted line. He did say that you may well be offered other trades when you come to the selection board But it will be up to you if you want another choice. My course was set. Six guineas a week and half again as marriage allowance. They weren't giving you anything, that's what is cost them to 'board' a single man.

HAYLING ISLAND

While waiting for the call to join I took a job at Yacht haven Northney on Hayling Island in the paint shop. I had to cycle from Iping but it was late Spring and there we refurbished yachts for wealthy owners. Mischoo? the painter took me under his wing and showed me how to apply Gold Leaf. Allowed me to put a finishing coat on a vessel. The prep, rubbing down and paint mixing were all part of it. i.e. an owner might come in with a stone or tobacco tin and want his yacht in that colour. We had a motor torpedo boat in and Mischoo said it belonged to a Lloyd's underwriter. What's one of them? Even when explained I didn't understand. I understood all right when painting it and a hand appeared out the porthole clutching a large Whisky. Too soon to give it up. My papers had come through. I was to report to Cardington in Beds for induction into the Royal Air Force. 20 June 1960. Summer and the Sun shone. Cardington was where they built Airships in the thirties and the huge hangers were still there.

We were taken about by a very polite oldish corporal. Would we come this way? That way. 1st stop medical. Strip to the buff and pirouette in front of three doctors. I was patchy like a Piebald horse. Is that your suntan peeling off asked one. Yes I say. The last doctor at the pool said I had tropical ringworm, but that smelly stuff he gave me never worked. Noses were looked up, chests sounded. Well we passed. The hearing test was to stand at the end of a thirty foot hut facing the wall. The medic would whisper a word while approaching one. Time I heard it he was practically touching me. As I was a regular and not National Service I was deemed fit. (fate again?). Next job was kitting us all out and shipping off home our civvies. End of the week, please clean your bed space and tomorrow we entrain for Bridgenorth and Basic training. Boot Camp!

BRIDGENORTH

Up in Shropshire. The camp motto was Havec Porta Moeni Viris. This is the gate, the walls are men. Once off the train we were bussed to camp where we were met by these corporals yelling and screaming. Off the bus. Line up! Hurry yourselves. Coo what a change. Boot camp. We were about thirty to a hut, two huts I think. It was square bashing, how to march, turn, look airmanlike etc. Lectures on the R.A.F. more selection boards, medicals, how to fire a rifle: which I had a talent for. Got a marksman's badge for my efforts. And drill; lots of it. More importantly how to fill in a leave pass. I got a forty-eight hour pass and went home for the weekend. Coach to Portsmouth and we went down the M1 with barely a car in sight. Bit of a change from today. Every night, bull your kit. Boots to a high shine, webbing blancoed. Kit inspections. Ones bed was to be made up each day and a blanket pack built. Blanket sheet, blanket sheet, blanket pillow slips all wrapped round with a blanket and squared up. Any not conforming were thrown out the hut window by the D.I.'s. Drill Instructors. You were issued with a mug, china, white for the use of. Knife fork and spoon. There were hot water tubs outside the mess for washing your own. 1st man in the wash-house ripped out the plug so it was down the NAAFI and buy one. There was a NAAFI on camp where you could get tea and a wad but lack of cash and the need to continually bull one's kit usually put paid to that. If you had to go anywhere alone say headquarters even the S.A.C's would yell at you. They were there to help and process one. Human bloody nature. But we survived. At last after six-weeks it was pass out parade and we were deemed ready to go on to trade training. The hut was full of excitement and speculation re the morrow and it was nearly the morrow when I got up and wiped the floor with the lot of them. Like kids at Christmas they couldn't stop talking about the next day. Then we all got a bit of kip. Off on our travels the next day armed with a railway warrant and all my kit I was off to RAF Locking near Weston Super Mare for my training.

R.A.F. LOCKING No1 radio school
motto Thorough

The gate on Locking Moor Road leads through the headquarters buildings and the parade square and fell away down to four huge blocks that were the training classes and then wooden huts for the troops. There were several hundred off us. National Service was coming to a close and new adult entries were needed to fill the gaps. Locking also housed an apprentice wing, well separated from us.

One was processed by a sergeant and allocated bedding

and a hut. I was to be on Pool flight (rent a bod) until my course Ground Radar Mechanic started in a couple of weeks. I was issued to the carpenters section to help out as and when. There was a chap repairing a Land rover who was a Coppersmith by trade. I was then moved to help a chippie to make some steps to surmount a pipe run. But soon enough we were classed up and GRM56 started. An ex Flight Sergeant just retired was the instructor. I of course forget his name. He was good to us and halfway through the course he took us round to his house for tea and a look at his Austin-Healey 3000. So we learned about Ohms Law and how electronics worked in the days of Thermionic valves. We also did maths and English for the RAF education tests 1&2. The blackboard carried the class title, instructors name and CCF. Class Chuff factor. Days done over days to do. Thus the greater the No. the nearer to finishing.

One of the lads Derek?? had a car. Hillman and we could get off camp. Usually down to the front at Weston Super Mare and the Four Roses Cafe where we listened to Roy Orbison who seemed to be flavour of the month. Weekends would see us farther afield visiting Wells or even Stonehenge. (No visitor centre; just stroll in). But all to soon we were awaiting our first posting. We'd filled a form in stating our preferences and nearly all had opted for Eastbourne where there was a Radar. I thought maybe as it was oversubscribed as it were I'll go for Suffolk, Norfolk and Lincs. In the event I got North Coates nr Grimsby. One lad got Saxa Vord which is about as far North as you can get without falling off the edge as it were. The instructors last posting had been North Coates and he said I would enjoy it and to tell Sqn. Ldr Malarkey that he was settled in and doing well.

I arrived there just before Christmas and as the place had closed down virtually for the holiday I was issued some bedding and placed in transit for ten days or so.

Fortunately Bob from Hitchin was in the same boat and a sort of friendship sprung up between us. Finally the RAF came back to work and I was assigned to No.1 Fire Unit. The station was a front line Bloodhound Unit. There being three 'units' each having sixteen missiles. A search Radar on the airfield and two type 83 Radars for the missile tracking. Flt Lt Dolman was in charge with a warrant officer Harry Dove, sergeant Jim Green and two corporals. Norman Reeves and Brian Pavey. There was a couple of mechanical types next door and a corporal to each T83 and about six operators. SAC's who did little but sit in the tin hut outside and drink tea and play cards. Norman took me under his wing and showed me how things worked until I was competent to do the simpler jobs.

Basically the search Radar 'found' the targets, the T83 illuminating Radar fed the chosen co-ordinates to the controller who picked a missile, pressed the tit and bingo. Well that was the theory.

I was absorbed in the newness of it all. I found a place to rent in Sixhills street Grimsby £3 a week and installed Betty and Jackie. Walked for the bus in the morning stopping for a paper. I took the Mirror like home but changed to the Express. Up the bus station to get old Tom's bus to camp. We had very little money left each week if any and for a diversion we'd go for a walk. Everyone seemed to have an Aspidistra in the parlour window. Window shop. We never even had a radio. I even made Jackie a dress of sorts. Betty never complained and though I was acutely aware of our plight I could do nothing.

My mum came to visit and left us a fiver which we brought a radio with. Heaven. Then they closed Binbrook. Binbrook was a flying station on the Wolds about twenty miles away. I was offered a married quarter there. Rent 27/- a week and fully furnished even down to the mustard spoon. The chap leaving it left it like a new pin. When you took a quarter the families officer was present,the barrack warden, and the inventory was checked down to the last detail, and, the cleanliness. We moved in which left us some spare cash. We could even go to Grimsby and the pictures. Mind you we had to leave before the end to catch the last bus back. Then somebody said: your entitled to disturbance allowance. What's that? As you've moved residences, I was up accounts like a shot. Can I? NO said the warrant, piss off. Hatch opened; officer i/c said yes he is. Do it. I was throw a form. Fill that in. I took it back to the Fire Unit and we all poured over it. Selected place of residence public accommodation, selected place of residence private accommodation. We got it filled in eventually and I collected £25 disturbance money. Boy was Betty pleased. We got the bus to Louth that weekend and had a lovely spend-up!

R.A.F. BINBROOK

Binbrook was up a rather steep hill, but there was a pub at the bottom and a chippie with coal fired pans. Lovely fish and chips. I could also afford to have one night a week in the pub. Domino's with Wrigley. There was little enough to do. A paper, a bus to Louth. Next door to watch telly. Her husband was away and she never minded us going in to watch. For Christmas we would gather Jackie and the presents and go down to Iping Avenue for the festivities and then drag all the way back up there (rail and bus) in the New Year. Heavy snow one year and the service bus which used to collect us for work each day; couldn't get up the hill. Cars were sliding about on the hill and one lad stepped in to help and straight on his arse and slid down the hill.

To earn a shilling or two we got a job lifting Sugar Beet. You cut the tops off the things so the farmer could do the bizzo and then followed along behind picking them up and throwing then in the cart. It was bitterly cold. We were four and it was £4 an acre. I asked the farmer how big an acre was and he was amazed I didn't know. He did appear next day with a chain and measured it. I fancy we only done a week. Gave it up. Too cold. And the kids all day wrapped in push chairs. Hopeless.

Back in Pompey I had acquired a James Cadet motorcycle took it round to my mate Jake Witcher, full of joy. He promptly stripped the engine down, (two stroke) and pointed out the big end was knackered. I took the big end back to the shop and they repaired it. The thing ran but it was never right, My first buying of the dog on the lot. I've got A levels in it. And have ever since. On a good day I'd take it to work at the Fire Unit. If it was a Friday I'd ask the W.O. Harry Dove could I nip off early and go to Grimsby to pay my never never before Binbrook. He would say to me sometimes at work. Lend me your paper. I won't do your crossword. I'd attempt it lunchtimes and Harry would cough it off in the P.M. I gone to work on the motor-bike one time and the return journey was made in the pouring rain and me with my service issue showerproof mac. Boy was I wet. I got sick passing broken glass and barbed wire. They put me in Nocton Hall, an RAF Hospital. Gave me a Iodine to light the tubes to X-rays and gave me a Cystofscopy. Pills to fix. I worked it out later. I'd been carrying a pool of cold rain between my legs and chilled my bladder to the bone.

I approached M.T. to see if I could get a class C licence to drive on the airfield. The sergeant said get in the Landrover and show me what you can do. Well the camp roads were designed for three men abreast and all the corners were right angles. I was all over the place. You'll do he say and I got my first RAF form 1629. That meant I'd collect a Landrover from MT in the am. and drive to the fire unit. Ostensibly it was for collecting water.

The RAF operated a warm body scheme for about everything. Station Duties they called it. Fire piquet. It was a week living in the Fire section with the full time airmen/firemen. There were lectures on fire. (surprise). Nuclear, Biological and Chemical warfare. These were given by a dry stick of a sergeant. The trouble was, North Coates being a high tech station there were more chiefs than Indians and the fire piquet came round monthly along with the same bloody lectures. Then some bright spark had a fire engine on standby at the actual fire unit. I spent a weekend with two wooden firemen. I hadn't thought to bring a book. I spent the time painting a board depicting the RAF Bloodhound Crest.

Our fireman Wrigley got me and him a job at the funfair in Cleethorpes on the candy and popcorn stall. He had a Vespa scooter but because he didn't have a licence I drove the scooter. Wrigs was huge married to a Dutch girl. Had a full licence for the camp fie engine. Funny enough we had a fire. Officers Mess. Fag end in armchair, smouldered all night. Time the real Fire Brigade got there from Grimsby some C.O. type officer broke a window letting the air in and woosh. Total loss. Talking of fire. There was a little wooden church on site and it was my turn to light the coke stove to warm the place. I was on piquet duty again. It was November. Where's the kindling? No kindling just use paper. I tried but no chance. When I left the fire was smouldering and the place was full of smoke. No draught either. Dank, airless November day.

I'd been to sick bay and complained about my 'Tropical Ringworm'. They discovered what it was but wouldn't treat it as too expensive. I waited for Doc Church who was the locum when the RAF doc was on holiday. Come into the dispensary he say. We'll start on the top shelf and work our way along. About three along it cleared up a treat and has never come back. Then suddenly a fitters course. Twelve months training. So pack up the family. Hand over the quarter and back to living with Ma Logie.

R.A.F. COMPTON BASSET No. 3 Radio School.

The course from mechanic to fitter was available because the National Service entrants were finishing their two years and leaving. Lucky for me! We should have been at RAF Locking but because much building was going on it was Compton. Just down the road from Calne and opposite the White Horse (in Chalk). There were thousands of us. Here we made some long term relationships. Well one had to over nine months in class. Mick Mc Cormick, Kevin Mac cormack, Marty Baldwin and a dozen others. It was all theory with a little lab work from time to time. I didn't get home often due to the shortage of money. Most nights Mick and I played snooker. I never won. I did one night and Mick threw his cue against the wall. We never played again. Winter was upon us and there were two pot bellied stoves in the hut situated about a third in. Mick and I would forgo NAAFI break and top up the coke supply for our stove Nobody bothered with the other one and when out would all crowd round our one. Lazy sods!

Marty Baldwin was an ex Bristol bus conductor. He'd won a scholarship to college but had been seduced by an older woman and lost it. Both his 'cherry' and the scholarship. He sat at the back of the class reading science fiction. One time Corporal Longbottom, the instructor, who had just chalked up the formulae for positive feedback from the manual; leapt on Marty asking him what was on the blackboard. Marty screwing up his eyes to see said. As a formulae it won't work unless you put the minus sign at the bottom and promptly went back to his book. The instructor checked the book and his copying. Seems the manual was wrong.

Every few weeks there was a slip test to see if any knowledge had gone in. Marty usually finished first and would have a screwed up copy of his answers which would be dropped on Mick's desk. He'd copy it and pass it on.

There were half a dozen blokes getting his answers and they made sure they didn't all get the same mark. No one ever discovered the ruse. So we progressed with AC theory, thermionic valves, flip flops, radios and oscillators. Crumbs did it go on. In the Radio lab I had access to a signal generator which I used to measure my hearing. Left ear cut out at about 10.5 Kilohertz and the right ear made about 11. Basically half the audio spectrum. Mastoids at fifteen.

Wednesday afternoon was sports afternoon. The Medical branch degreed that students needed to run about in the fresh air. Our lot made there way down the local pub and after a few beers back to the billet and a snooze. Wonderful. The Powers that be became aware of this practise and one Wednesday lined us all up outside HQ. Right who's for football? Off you go. Rugby? Swimming? Bicycle club? Then we were hundred plus. Right follow the PTi to the Gymnasium. Time the PTi got to the gym he had about six blokes left. They'd all melted away between the billets. Next Wednesday the authorities being aware of last weeks debacle, went through the usual routine and the with sentries every few yards marched us out the main gate saying don't come back 'til five o' clock. So after a few pints it was sneak back into camp time.

Twas the Winter of 62/63. I'd been home to Betty and had got the train back as far as Cheltenham when I heard that the camp was closed due to heavy snow. I rang the guardroom and said I was having difficulties getting back. and they confirmed. Return home and await a telegram. Which I needed no second telling. Those that had managed to return were put in snow clearing duties. Not a happy crowd. It wasn't long before the extended break was over, but the snow hung about for weeks. They put Aladdin oil heaters in the ablution blocks to hold off the pipes freezing. Wing Commander Wiley said anyone thinking of removing them to get another holiday had another think coming.

Nobody would get off camp. Frozen or not. One bloke was found with six round his bed!

The car we travelled home in on weekends (share the petrol) had no heater and the freeze was still on. He wired a tin round the exhaust pipe stuffed with wire wool and a pipe into the car. Not very effective. Shame. Schooling went on, and the little tests; then we were due for the big one covering all that had gone before. Muggings gets the Flu and goes special sick. You could only go sick before 8am. They took me to Yatesbury (No 2 Radio school). and stuck me in sick bay for a week. Back for the exam: failed it! We are in front of the wingco and he say. Fail again and the RAF will decide what trade you should be in. Think about it.

We had a very large man in our hut. Woodbine. Well he went AWOL and was missing for a few weeks. When he finally re-appeared, he said he'd fallen in love and only wanted to be with her. The officer i/c asks. How did you manage without money? I didn't he say I came back each week for pay parade. Time you got to the 'w's there weren't many left. Well who paid you? You did sir! Ouch.

Betty was pregnant again. Whoopee, Colin was on the way and this time my insistence that she go into hospital for it met with no demur. We took Betty down to St. Mary's when she was due and because of the problems having Jackie, the hospital were aware of the Toxaemia/Eclampsia problems. To take my mind off it, Joyce and Ron took me to Bognor for the day. When I rang the hospital and found out we had a boy I was down there straight away. What do you think of your son asked the nurse. He's Ace I replied.

We were due to shift to RAF Locking for the practical part of the course, so I put an ad in the Weston Mercury for some rooms and got a reply. Once we'd made the move I went and inspected them. Top floor of a nice stone house backing on to the cemetery. Had a word with Andy Brewster who had a Ford Thames van and he drove me to

Iping. (no phones in those days). And after a quick stop in Fareham where his dad ran the chemist and it was! Surprise surprise at 11 Iping. Get your kit together we have rooms in WSM. Promptly loaded the pram and Colin in the back with me. Betty in the front with Jackie and back to WSM.
I fancy Mrs Logie was quite pleased to get her home back.

The practical side of training was more satisfying being hands on affair, though some of the old kit was lethal: particularly the Console 61. Mind you so many trainees had worked on it finding faults it was a wonder it held together.
Sometimes the two paddy's would come round and ask Betty if they could take her man up the pub. Starkey's bitter 1/4 a pint. (7p). We discovered that Kevin was Kevin Ignatius and after that was known as big Iggy.

We had the usual mix of practical, some theory and parades. About once a month full kit all shined and polished. I fancy it was more for the C.O.'s benefit, but it had to be done: and those short of kit for one reason or another and couldn't do the parade had the discip Flt. Sgt. Follet coming round class on Tuesday saying Wednesday 10am Officer i/c. On a charge and on jankers. Easier to keep one's kit together. Haggis came to me one day saying you've got kids, my wife and I have been trying for ages but no joy. Well I say try the Catholic Rhythm method. We're trying to have kids not not have. Yes I say. Turn it on it's head. Instead of screwing your brains out every opportunity, tie a knot in it and wait until she ovulates: then try! Worked a charm.

Eventually we passed the finals tests and were posted to new units. The Irish to Bishops Court to a man and me back to North Coates. The Fire Units had gone and there was only 148 wing repair and maintain, which is where they put me. There was a flight sergeant. Two senior techs and a couple of corporals. Me, dogsbody. A least I was now a junior technician. The Flt Sgt said I shouldn't be there.

Meaning North Coates. But they gave us a quarter and we moved in toot sweet. The place was running down as they were phasing out the Bloodhound system. There was some work but mostly they had us smashing up the printed cct boards with a sledge hammers to reduce them as much as possible before sending them to the furnaces in Sheffield. As the place was closing down we all filled in our choice of posting forms. i.e. where would you like to serve next? I was with a work party outside headquarters when a clerk came out and handed me a railway warrant and said . Go to RAF Buchan now. What now? Yes this minute! Don't be silly, I need time to tell the missus. Pack and get ready. They gave me three days. It appears that while on the fitters course records office had posted me to Buchan, but they forgot to tell me; and having returned me to North Coates, someone, (other than the Flt Sgt) should have queried it with records the moment I walked through the door. I bet somebody's head rolled. Shame we were settled in to life on the quarters and made a friend or two The woman next door used to be more often than not because I had a box (gross) of condoms, and she'd be in to borrow a few. Nice lass, common as muck, but good company. Had Christmas there, save lugging everything back to Leigh Park and back again. Ma and Pa Logie came to visit. There's a first. Got themselves a puppy from someone on the patch They'd gone by Christmas and we cashed our NAAFI dividend for six beers and a bottle of wine. Had a chicken and a tin of Old Oak Cooked Ham. Thought we were well set up. The booze was shared with Corporal Parkinson. the condom lady's hubby. He invited his sergeant in for a drink as the sergeant had loads in his place. The sergeant drank a bottle of beer and then went home. No return invite So we were one beer down. Ho Hum!

So here I am booted up to Buchan. Out of the train at Aberdeen and over to the bus station for the thirty mile trip to Boddham near Peterhead. The bus dropped me outside the Rocksley pub in the dark early evening. I walked to the guardroom where the snowdrop (RAF Police) said. Oh your tech are you? Right lot of boozers. Oh I thought this place looks better already. I was issued bedding and assigned to an eight man billet. Report in the morning. One went round all the people that might have an interest in one as a way of arriving as it was called. Boddham was the domestic site and the Radar was up the hill a couple of miles away. The work hours were 8-1. 5-10 three days the 1-5 and 10-8. Day or two off. So one went in twice a day. Suited Ops, Tech wanted their own hours but MT wouldn't have it. The next problem was finding somewhere to live. Betty couldn't stay in quarters overlong, but there was nowhere. People lived in what they had and there was no letting market. The families officer suggested I try Annie Murrays guest house just outside the gate.

They were building new quarters, but a a lowly J/T I was never going to have enough points to qualify for one. I went to see Annie. Large roly poly woman. Yes! She'd have us at eight pounds a week. Full board of course. I told Betty and she agreed it was better than nothing, or living with mum! The drawback being that again I'm learning a new skill, and enjoying the social intercourse one gets at work and she'd be stuck with sod all to do and nowhere to do it in. Having the kids helped.

Annie's man had just retired and in the barn was a load of sacking where Addie the odd job man slept. There was a bit of a garden where the ole boy grew taters, and there was ever a pot of porridge on the Aga. Annie had plenty of visitors and apart from another RAF family moving in it was fairly quiet. Night shifts on the Radar. The lads' would come off the afternoon shift, repair to the Rocksley and back to camp for supper and the bus up for the night shift. Cup of tea, game of bridge and- you have the con James. And retire somewhere for the night. Leaving me manning the phones and setting up the kit before making tea in the am. There was a sergeant who did days. Piggy Keeling. Odious sort. Two search radars, two height finders: all known as 'heads' There was a photographic display unit which displayed the radar picture on a plotting table. It could process film in three minutes. There was a civilian in charge of that, another on heads and one in second line and another looking after the display equipment known as the radar office. All underground. But the airmen were keen and could do the job. Civvies gave continuity.

One day Annie said to me The gardener at the Ugie hospital has been made up to head man and gets a tied cottage with the job. He'd like to rent his bothy out at Burnhaven. Do you want to see it? So with no more ado we went and looked 6 High Street Burnhaven. Just up from the beach. High Street because it was above Low street which was about on the beach. Peterhead prison sat above it and the Long John Distillery the other end. The place was of Granite, three rooms a bit of a hall and a long lean-to on the front which acted as a kitchen with running water; cold. The loo (chemical) was outside alongside the defunct washhouse. It boasted a garden running down to the sea and a large shed affair. Four quid a week. We jumped at it. The landlord, forgotten his name gave us a little cash book the type you could buy in Woolworths. That I was to take to the Clydesdale? bank in Peterhead and give them the rent which would be entered in my little book. The money in the bank was lying on the large table behind the counter.

We got our furniture sent up; what there was of it and settled in. There was a shop at the main road and a school where Jackie started her education. Straight in, no playing trouble was in a few weeks she was using the local dialect and we couldn't understand her. It was about now that we noticed her eye problem that was diagnosed as a lazy eye and was covered over to improve same. There was a picture of us leaving with Betty holding a kettle and Jackie with her plastered glasses. Colin had baby Eczema but that cleared up once we'd converted the dosage from metric to imperial. In this part of Scotland one had Loons and Queans. Boys and girls.

Life was good. I was getting a good grounding in my trade. Some days they would ask me to go down to the remote type7 Radar and run it up for the calibration run. This was an early radar with the gubbins underground. One entered via a flat hatch. Lecobar Oscillators operating at about 209Mhz and twin feeders as opposed to waveguide. One locked the Aerial with an Iron bar on a reflector while you tuned the kit for maximum signal. They gave it up after a year. Shame it was a good day out in Summer.

We had the odd trip to Aberdeen, funds permitting. There was a Typhoid scare from contaminated Argentine beef and the RAF sent us (not families') to Aberdeen for Immunisation. There was fishing and farming and that was about it. Alexander's buses only employed clippies but as soon as they wed they were sacked. They then had a man to support them. Made sense at the time.

Buchan was from the locals point of view a marriage farm. The amount of single men there that attracted the local lasses. We seemed to marry one a week. Browns hotel in Peterhead was the Friday night venue. If I got an opportunity to go I was pointedly ignored as they knew I was married. Once the lads had been paid and been up Brown's hotel or the Seaview pub in Boddham our little shed became a popular watering hole. We couldn't afford to feed the buggers. They all had healthy appetites. But it was where a few regulars were glad to get off camp when broke. Bill Ranson spent hours with me wandering the beach. He was one of my shift partners and we became firm friends. Marty Baldwin was another. He was acky. Lend me a shirt so I can go out. You've already got two of mine. Oh, well I'll just wash the collars and cuffs on this one. He met and married Elle. I can't get it in! Well wait until I've got my knickers off. Bill did most of his courting at our place. Pat had a very keen father who was a prison officer and wasn't having any daughter of his getting in the family way. My mum came to visit and we took her round the lighthouse at Boddham. She enjoyed that. Brother Arp and wife Sandy drove all the way up from Hayling Island and stayed a couple of nights. Only took eighteen hours. Brother Michael came as he was in the Tug-o-War team representing the RAF at the Braemar games. I was in the Tug-o-War team in the Tech verses Ops on out annual sports event. Baz a large coloured man came, just arrived. still in uniform and threw the Discus out of sight. Tech won and I got a pewter tankard. Any one leaving on posting would have a leaving do in the Seaview Hotel in Boddham and he'd put us in the back room as soon as they had a pint in their hands as they all wanted to sing. Rugby type songs. I hated it.

Bill Ranson decided we should go shooting Rabbits for the pot. Pigeons too. I went the Post Office and bought a gun licence for 10/-, then to the station armoury and borrowed a shotgun. Bill got the shells. And a gun likewise. He'd cleared the 'hunt' with a farmer and off we went. I think I got one and Bill a couple. The guns were left behind the settee. It was that easy. I got myself a bike to ride to camp for the bus up to site and someone nicked it. Going to the Police station there were dozens to choose from.

We were young and had fun and worked hard. The ole boy next door had come all the way from Australia to bury his brother and never returned. The next next door where some Tinks. They had me fill their application form in to become club members of a catalogue and get a free saucepan. There was a keening one morning and she was out in the street with her baby. Dead! I held it and it was cold and wet. Infant death syndrome. I went to the funeral as a neighbourly thing to do. Women in Scotland didn't attend funerals. The other child only seemed to have a vest even outside. I said to Betty. Can't you give her some of Jackie and Colins cast offs? No point said Betty she only sells them and buys booze.

Ritchie the postman showed me how to catch Lobsters with a hooked broom handle. He would take Colin at three fishing with him. They'd sit on the harbour Mole. Frightens the life out of me thinking about it now. They asked me to be M.C. for some reason at the Tech Do at the Palace hotel. Not that I had any idea what was expected of me. Make a bit of a speech someone said, and that seemed to go down well. Then I'm dancing with Pat.(Bills intended) and she say to me. What's it like? Well your here you tell me. No she say not this.THAT. Oh! Waking up to her meaning. Well I'm hardly in a position to tell you. You could always show me she say. Come New Year found me in the Palace hotel at the dance with half bottle of Whisky. The place closed at 9:30 pm and we all went up the town square to wait for midnight. When the clock struck everyone was kissing and hand shaking and wishing all a Guid New Year. Then first footing. Anywhere there was a lit house, bang on door and enter: present your Whisky and have a drink leave and repeat the process elsewhere. Glad I did it for the experience.

Mother was now a laundress on the Caronia which was visiting Edinburg so I trained down to Edinburg
and found where the liberty boats were coming ashore. Said to the officer. My mum's on the boat. Can I go out and see her. Yes he say. Spent a few hours with her. Nice. Wouldn't happen today. She told me once while working for Union Castle that in Durban she met a Shaman,who said to mum. 'You have a man standing by your right shoulder who cares about you'. 'He wears a flat cap.' 'There is another man standing by your left shoulder who is worried about time'. Granddad if you asked him the time, would consult his pocket watch, wind it a few times and

then consult it some more. She may have guessed the flat caps but time?

Back on shift and Mick came in, a long faced lugubrious chap. I thought you were on a conversion course to 'heads'. How can I go he say. I've got seven kids. No wonder he had a long face. I was straight round to see the boss to arrange to go in his place. It was three months at Locking again and Betty would have to stay in the cottage. It was about now that the RAF decided that pay parades were a thing of the past and we would be paid by BACS. Monthly! One could have a loan and pay it off over four pay-days. I went for that and informed the Landlord that he would get his rent at the end of the month. And I was off to Locking (again). Fate now took hand.

Having arrived and got sorted for bed and bedding went off to the 'school' and reported in. Ah! Yes say Flt Sgt. Gregory, I knew you were coming late but there's another bloke missing. Name of Azzaro. Will you see if you can find him? Where am I going to find some foreign bloke when there's 800 plus of us here? Just forget it.

We were in the new built blocks with four man rooms. and single ones for the junior NCO's I went looking for an iron and found this bloke ironing a shirt; starkers. Azzaro! Yes John always late or bucking the system. Determined to go his own way and like all rebels in a disciplined society well regarded. At the end of course I fancy John seven. RAF two! Tuesdays and the discip man Flt Sgt Follet would poke his head in the classroom and say: Azzaro, boss tomorrow ten hundred hours, on a charge. Parker escort. So our fates were linked. I was called in front of the boss. Why was I not paying the rent? The landlord had complained. I explained that the new banking arrangements were the glitch and we left it there. The landlord got his rent as agreed. Finally end of course and back to Patrington for John and Buchan for me and Betty and the kids. Colin was coming along fine and we still couldn't understand

Jackie.

And I was still paying off Betty's slate at the shop when I got my baccy. Newly qualified I was assigned to 'heads' and after a spell on days was put on shift as the type 80 driver. The RAF assigned numbers to their Radars roughly as they came into service. The type 80 (Decca) was the main search head and the J.T. looking after it the-driver.

There were two search heads and three? Height finders being ANFPS6 American radars. Night shift saw me and Alan Laverty looking after the lot. Both about twenty. We must have been doing something right as the station won the Ingpen Trophy or best serviceability. Small bronze figure of a nude winged man, arms aloft. Taff Gregor always on jankers was ordered to polish it prior to presentation. He did and it's genitalia was polished to a high shine. Taff said he'd spilt a drop of metal polish on it. The trophy was being presented by the wing commanders wife in all it's shining glory. When it appeared in the trophy cabinet it had acquired a Royal Stewart Tartan Kilt.

Bill Ranson came to me full of woe. He'd been posted: type 85 course RAF Locking, and what should he do about Pat? He could hardly court her from WSM. Simple Bill marry the girl and take her with you. So we had a wedding and a bit of a do afterwards and they left for Locking. A few months later and I was going myself.

Digital Computer Fundamentals course in the new five block. We were seventeen with fifteen expected to pass and two for wastage. The RAF was moving into the Digital age It was about three weeks on Venn Diagrams, Boolean Algebra and Binary. There was a computer in a lab the size of a very large cupboard. Thermionic valves. Access was restricted because someone was doing the Chinese alphabet or some such thing. Bit of cheek considering it was for training purposes. The class was Bill Sydenham, Fatty Turner, Alec Wells, Norman Coyne, Tony Dennet, Bloosy Morris, Ken Weston and Azzaro.

So time to give notice o the bothy at Burhaven, another airman moved in straight away so the gardener/landlord was happy. Mind you I heard he died of Testicular cancer, poor sod. I went in to admin to arrange travel warrants etc. The clerk was doing the business when a hatch opened and a voice said. He's not entitled. Not entitled? I'm posted! Yes said the voice. Posted RAF West Drayton, detached RAF Locking thus your family don't qualify. My boss got involved but the best offer was a loan from the C.O.'s fund. I wasn't having that. So what to do? In the end a bloke called Glen Rackstraw whom I'd kept in fags while on fire piquet offered to drive us to Emsworth. (staying with my mum) for £10 to cover the petrol. I had little choice and we accepted. He overnighted at mum's and didn't seem in any hurry to go off to Manchester. We persuaded him in the end. So Betty and the kids settled into Record Road. Mum was at sea and only brother Arthur was living there so there was room. I went off to Locking.

Bill and Pat had settled into the upstairs rooms at Mrs. Roberts in Garsdale road near the Borough Arms. I of course went round to see them. Pat was in one of those see-through negligee things ex bath. Bill had got himself a job at the Borough Arms, barman, and was about off. Stay and chat with Pat I'll be back later. I don't think so Bill she'll have me in bed before your backs turned. We'll all go down the pub and have a drink.

Sitting at the table and Pat's saying we did it in the Sleeper from Aberdeen three times and I loved it, and, what did I think of girls that take it in the mouth? One can only take so much temptation. I stayed the night at Bill's insistence. Mrs Roberts had a truckle bed in the loft. Next morning I am waiting on the bus on the Locking Moor road and a car stops. it's Sgt Wells. (Alec). Get in he say I thought I recognised you. The start of another lifelong friendship. Alec was on the same course but he and Sally were living in private accommodation and mere corporals didn't move in the same circles as SNCO's

We fell into the usual pattern at Locking. Down the town and try and get laid or for a drink, depending on your preferences. Me for the booze. Arranging lifts home for the weekend or hitch-hiking. Could take hours. Monday night camp stack as the cinema was known Tuesday was bridge club which John and I went as partners unless he was on Jankers. Thus an even closer bond was formed. We also shared a desk in class. The course was enjoyable. They took us to Bristol one night for a lecture by a man on Linesman Mediator by a man that more than knew his business. I'd still see Bill from time to time but avoiding Pat made it easier to stay away. Oh! I fancied her but she was Bill's missus. They were building quarters at west Ruislip and furnishing them in the latest G-plan style. Betty and I were allocated one along with Fatty Turner (next door) Pete Morris, Alec and Sally. The rest we allocated at Cowley near Yiewsley. Betty and I took a trip up to West Ruislip just to have a look. Impressed.

Once we'd finished the course and we arrived at West Drayton the Marconi, Plessey and Kelvin Hughes contractors were not ready for us, so they put us in a room while they wondered what to do. So visits were arranged. We did the National Physical Laboratory, where the bouncing bomb was tested. Fords at Laleham (lorries) and British Airways. Yes we will order Jumbo's when they are ready. Eventually we got into the L1 building as it was called and began work with the contractors. We were viewed as nuisance value at first but perseverance won the day and at last we were accepted. We were to do the Marconi equipment. Amazing, there were these engineers doing the business with complete confidence. They were buying houses at Wallingford and the like and getting £25 a week maintenance: never mind their salary! My pay was £18 take home. But we were soon learning the equipment and being invited to parties with them. We played them at football and cricket at the local council sports grounds. After a drink at the local pub it was over to terminal two for coffee. Crazy, super, whatever. There were no facilities at West Drayton from the RAF point of view. One Warrant Officer. An admin clerk. A dozen RAF policemen and M.T. with a couple of buses. There was a site canteen and we segued into civilian life seamlessly.

R.A.F. WEST DRAYTON

We were to be screened as in the new digital age we wouldn't be posted for a least five years, which gave us a bit of chance to put down, if not roots exactly but a bit more settled Schools at Ruislip. We even started to attend the local church. As the camp was in the hands of the builders there were no NAAFI canteens, or messes. They gave us the old station church so we could have a families club which was for all ranks: canteen/bar/ what have you. We advertised in the local press for furniture donations to which they responded well. Me and Bloosy were round to two old ladies who were giving us a couple of settees. They felt that at least an invitation when opened, which we assured them they'd get. Never happened as we were appropriating them for ourselves. Having people living at Ruislip and Cowley being a dozen miles and half a dozen made it very difficult to get people to come. We tried running a cinema. The kit was supplied by the Army Kinematic Society along with the films; but it flopped. So we gave that up. Then someone started a bar in a spare room. We looked in once but it wasn't good. Couple of times a week Alec and Sally would come over and ask Betty if they could take me up the pub. We used the Fox and Geese at Ickenham. I was to get a job there. Thus a friendship between us was developing. Money was tight being a London posting and we were waiting to get

'London weighting' on top of our wages.

Coming back from the swing park Colin fell off his bike and broke his arm and I'm saying stop being a baby it can't hurt that much. It was the next day before Betty had him up the hospital. Greenstick fracture of the Ulna. It was that same swing park that Nicola fell off the slide. Never did get to the bottom of that. From the top I understand now. Colin also contracted Scarlatina and was confined at home. The headmaster rang me to say it was a notifiable disease and why hadn't I? Well I didn't know. You do! So notify someone.

John Azzaro was getting married in Hull to Gwen and I was invited of course. Wether I was best man I can't remember. Perhaps his brother Peter. or, Pontius the Pilot as John called him. Peter being a captain on V bombers. A church in Hull being the venue. The Father had asked John where did he get his pre ceremony lectures? John of course replied Locking but I don't think the Father believed him and as Gwen wasn't Catholic he wasn't too bothered. We were in Church and Gwen was early so she went into a pub in all her finery. Once in the church the ceremony took just eight and a half minutes. So the priest wasn't wasting any time on this lot of unbelievers. There being little money about we repaired somewhere for a bit of a bun fight before the happy couple went off on honeymoon. Knowing I was going to be at a loose end I'd contacted Bill Ranson who was now serving at RAF Staxton Wold in Yorkshire and living in Bridlington. We would have a drink together and I would stay the night. Which we did. Bill was on earlies in the morning and said goodbye leaving me in the front room Difficult. I knew Pat was both willing and available but as Bill was my mate. So we stayed where we were. Once up I needed to go down the railway station and find out times of trains. Chance to walk the dog. Pat cooked me a bit of lunch but the atmosphere was strained because of the bed thing. Finally I was off and that was that.

It was about now that we took Jackie to Moorfields Eye hospital in Holborn for further investigation into her eye. After exhaustive tests they said that to cut the eye muscle to reduce the squint meant, if they got it wrong they couldn't correct it. And Jackie was now used to her 'squint' and would have trouble re-adjusting her sight. Best to leave it and better techniques in the future may hold a solution. So we did. Seeming the best option. Subsequently the advice was good. Lazer eye surgery was introduced but Jackie had to pay for it herself at some cost.

The next lot of quarters at Cowley were nearing completion and John and Gwen were in line to get one. Betty agreed that they could stay with us until the move. John had to clear it with the camp Adjutant in the shape of Flt. Lt. Jim Cornish. Yes one could obviously have visitors in married quarters providing it wasn't overlong. As John was leaving Jim Cornish said. Do you know anyone local you could use as an address when requesting permission to 'live out'? Wing Commander Watts an old family friend. Lives in Wembley. Right said Jim use that address and don't forget to claim home to duty expenses from there. Talk about aiding and abetting. Not that it was long. Fortunately Betty and Gwen got along famously so no friction in the kitchen. In those days John might even wash up. Not too often though.

Back to the families club again. It became a duty. A roster set up and we all had to take turns. Not happy. Even though they were paying £4 a week. I said to Bill Sydenham the chief. How about me and Azzaro doing it full time for the percent of the take? That was agreed and we were back in the 'church'. The local builders ganger came in to see if he and the men could drink in the place but No! Sorry. But after some chat it was agreed that he would provide hot pies, sausages in a roll and ham and cheese rolls for lunchtimes- delivered. The contractors as in Marconi, Kelvin-Hughes and Plessey found it a boon and in six weeks we had gone from £9 in the red, to £400 in the black. The C.O. was happy as his 'fund' was good. Of course we introduced some of our own stock to boost profits (ours) even further. After clearing up we might go down the Black Swan and have a Steak. Getting back in the evenings was a chore and John said to me; look, I'm at Cowley and your at Ruislip. Take my old Volks home and pick me up on the way back and again in the morning. How about insurance? I've checked your O.K. Your covered. The car was falling apart and was left hand drive and No, I wasn't covered by insurance. Fortunately, no accidents.

I'd had a bit of leave and returning to the Families club lunchtime found the door open and no one about. Popping in next door to the Fire Section I ask Eric what was going on. Fg Off John Thomas has closed you down for nefarious activities. Stock check at 1300hrs. Where's John? Down the Swan. I nip back in the club and remove the whisky and Gin that we supplied and Eric secretes them in his filing cabinet. Over to the L1 building see Chief Sydenham and asked him why the club was locked. He repeated what Eric had told me. So I hung about and we walked over to the club together and at the door I held my hand out for the key: which he gave me and I was able to rattle it in the lock before entering. John appeared and likewise Fg Off John Thomas. Taking the stock book he said to John, right we'll start with the Rum. Yes sir, Red or White? Don't get clever with me. Once it was pointed out that there was indeed both Red and White (clear) Rum he decided to do the beer. Several barrels were in store. The ones in use had to be weighed and the contents read off a scale in pints. Plus times all the other barrels in stock. Handing the book to John he say. You do the stock check. Your still closed though: you can send all the beer back. Yes say John but you'll only get a credit note for it. So John phones a certain Jim Cornish who was at Medmenham up the A4. Having appraised him of the situation, he asked. Is it money? No Sir. I didn't think so with you two. I've not been here very long but there's a pub in the village called the Dog and Duck I'll meet you there this evening. Going in John's old Volks we arrived at the said Dog and Duck and had a few with Jim Cornish while regaling him with all. We went back to his room in the Officers Mess for a nightcap and I'm trying on this Flt Lt's jacket. Then we were off. Yes well over the limit as usual.

There was a meeting about the club the next day in Fg Of Thomas's office. Strangely enough we were to be allowed to open the club again. Stricter rules of course. So the game was on again. It was coming up to Christmas and Plessey wanted the staff do in the club. Fixed budget and let us know when getting near. Of course in the pressure of serving the stuff and keeping a tab: extra drinks were added to the tally. Wicked I know but John was ever one to make a bob or two. Another was a dance for Xmas held in another building, which meant moving the bar across with the help of M.T. We'd rope Tony Dennett in as extra staff and away we went. Great Success, only trouble was that we'd had to move everything back after the dance. We did that for both dances and were up and running the next day. Of course we had to come in a bit later than start, but there wasn't much going on anyway work wise.

It was about now that a sea change occurred. For example a pub landlord got all his supplies from the brewery. Beer, wines, spirits, the lot. Annually this was all totted up and converted into Barralage and charge at two pence per barrel per annum. Then some smart brewery upstart said. Just a minute. We have 300 or so pubs and we're not charging any rent. They also turned money into a commodity. The RAF had leave clerks and accounts clerks. These were to be amalgamated. Watneys as well as Red barrel introduced Starlight. A near beer that was only good for flushing the system.

Come the New Year we packed the club in and returned to work proper. John with his determined way to be his own man fell foul of Mike Bradley. The senior Marconi engineer and was called to his office to explain himself. John told the Marconi man to piss off. John wasn't his man. Strangely Mike B became senior man in Jordan later but was killed in a car accident. and later still John became Mr Jordan when he worked with Marconi.

We set up a Duplicate Bridge club in the families club and that was quite popular. I took a job in the Fox and Geese at Ickenham. Mostly standing in the empty public bar and doing the odd customer in the half lounge. The other lounge was where John the landlord and Doris landlady sat
She was usually up to her eyeballs in gin and John was always having a nice Bass on his customers. He was an ex-diddycoy gypsy type. The roof of the cellar was thick with cobwebs. Then one day, none. I said crumbs John you've had a Spring clean. No he say health inspector. Don't know the half of it. There were lots of flies in the cellar next time down. See he say. Cobwebs control the flies.

About now I have to take Colin up to Leicester Square to the Dental Hospital for extractions under gas. When called in I could see that it had been done and quite brutal, but could find nobody about the place to complain to. So once he's recovered took him home. Reg Finch one in our lot who wasn't popular for no reason. We called him Knackers. He sold me his Morris six: ten pounds a month over four months. Lovely old bus. Six cylinders in line. Overhead cam. I loved it. Down to council offices at Ealing and get a drivers licence 15/-, simple. John and Doris were going on the last trip of The Queen Mary to the Azores and they got crooked Jack in to run the pub. He said to me one day. I see the car but have you passed your test? No I say. Well put in for it at Mill Hill and let me know when and you've passed. How? Ask no questions; just do it. So I did.

Come the day and it had snowed and the test was cancelled. Come the day of the next test and ten mins before the off to Mill Hill the water pump went on the Morris. This time Wellsey was my passenger. What a sod. Alec said to me. You can use my Cortina for the test, but don't tell Sally. Tell Sally? I wouldn't breathe a word. In spite of the odd trips up the pub and across to the mess I was in awe of Sally. Alec drove to the test centre and I had fifteen mins getting a feel for the Cortina. Then to the test centre. Once called and post number plate eye test, I said to the inspector I hadn't driven the car more than ten minutes and it wasn't mine anyway. In officialese he say to me. Are you satisfied for this vehicle for the purpose of the test? Humbled I replied yes and off we went. I rather thought I didn't do to badly. Come the theory bit we got in to trouble. I'd read the Highway Code but I didn't understand that he wanted me to tell him the difference between sign giving orders and those offering advice. In the end he say. You told me that this was not your choice of vehicle and were unused to it. I consider you drove it far too quickly and with Brio. Here is you pass certificate and got out and strode two yards to the kerb. Whoopee, over to Alec full of joy and on the way back we popped in the Starling at Hatch End for a celebratory glass. (was he crooked Jack's man?) I never advised him of the new test date and he'd left the pub anyway. I dunno to this day, but from his remarks it could well have been possible.

By now Janine was on the way. Janine? Carry on Cruising had a author on board and he wrote Janine.... I thought what a lovely French sounding Name.
Yes Arthur and Sandy had recently wed and we put it down to that. I was over the moon at the prospect of another child. Betty was under RAF Doctors and would go to RAF Halton nr Wendover in Bucks for her confinement. We had a Rover 90 then but more of that later.

Betty went in to RAF Halton for her confinement and

the popular song on the radio was. Joe Brown and the |
Bruvvers. Mrs Brown you've got a lovely daughter. The
morning off I went down the Post Office to collect the
child allowance. You can't collect it it's Mrs Parker's and
she hasn't countersigned it. I went over to the counter and
signed the back and foolishly returned to the same window.
Hoppit he say you can't sign it yourself. I'm her husband I
say, she is in Wendover with a baby and I have no money
for petrol. Tough, hoppit. I went wailing to Sally who
pointed out that she would have signed it, but lent me the
money for petrol. Racking up at visiting time to discover
that Mrs Brown did indeed have a lovely daughter.

Betty and I were at odds (surprise) over the care of the
quarter. Basically the R.A.F. expected you to live there but
never actually use the place. Bet's argument was that we
had kids and living meant a certain amount of mess. On
leaving a quarter one handed it over to the next tenant and
everything had to be ready to move in: like a newly
cleaned Hotel room. Not easy but people managed it O.K.
Bet got a job at the local bookies. Only cleaning at the end
of the day. She was sacked after a few weeks for failing to
do it. It was only up by the tube station.

I gave my notice in at the pub. Doris up to her
eyeballs in gin said stay behind after closing and tell me
why. She said to me. May comes in Fridays and Saturdays.
If a customer offers her a drink she says a shillings worth
of scotch, then has a full one anyway charging for the
shillings worth. Mo comes in lunchtimes and works her
way through crate of Worthington each week. Bruce does
Mondays and Wednesdays and helps himself to a packet of
fags each session. Why put up with it? Because I know
what they are doing and I can stand the loss. A new
member of staff would have me at a loss for a while.
Amazing. No I wasn't persuaded to stay.

We went to Ruislip Lido for a family day out.
Basically a large lake where people swim, sail, water-ski.

There is a sort of a wall alongside the swimming area. The Sun was shining and it was warm and I was feeling sleepy Colin wanted to go for a swim. He was about five or six at the time. I was loath to accompany him but thought I should. He was feeling his way along the wall and let go to move round this woman who had her feet in the water and promptly went under. I waited a couple of beats and jumped in and hauled him up. A great wail from Colin relieved my worries. The woman said to me I thought he was swimming. Good job I didn't give in to sloth!

One morning we were told to leave the L1 building and not return that day. Strange? No explanation given. The next day we were taken into a room in shifts handed pen and paper and told to write what was dictated by the security branch. It went~: I have a chronometer and it is set to go off. How do you spell chronometer? Just write it as you think.' The next day it was: read this message into the telephone for voice-printing. I was called round later to the room we'd been ringing to find an RAF copper listening to the messages. Where's the voice printer? We don't have one were just trying to see if we can match the callers voice. They were recording the calls. I went off and got a storage scope and fed the callers message in on one channel and the calls on the other trying to get a match. It was a bit hit and miss trying to get the timing right The RAF copper was more than impressed. He got me round to his place to fix his old telly.

The work installing the equipment was stalling with. Plessey wanting another two years. At the same time they were calling for volunteers to help out in M.T. (motor transport). To which John and I applied seeing a great scam. There were people living down the M4 at White Waltham, near Medmenham (The Compleat Angler) We were driving Austin J4 minibuses on loan from other units. Thus not of the best and in fact downright dangerous. The trouble was that our allocation of MT wouldn't kick-in until we became fully operational as a station. What a bloody stupid typical accountant type of idea. However if you were picking up at White Waltham one would tickle off early and call in the Barley Mow for a soft drink. (we weren't that silly) and sit with one's paper and crossword until pick-up time. I did have to take the C.O. to H.Q. Strike Command at High Wycombe for a C.O.'s conference. Pick-up RAF Uxbridge 07:30 driving down the A4 which was quite busy and a bit slow going. I started overtaking vehicles in the Austin 1800cc. I'd done a few when a motor-cycle cop pulled me. No don't stop he say. Your hedge-hopping, pack it in or I'll have you. Quelle embarrassment. At least I didn't crash it as one MT driver did with his C.O. So I'm sitting in the car idly looking through the paperwork. In every RAF vehicle there is and accident report form and written all round the envelope were chromimtre. chronemetter and so on. So the plot thickens. I told Archie the security officer later. Mmm! He say. We got the bugger. Silly pissed off airman. He was a bolshie piece of work anyway.

OTHER PURSUITS

Once we'd all settled in to quarters at West Ruislip the need to get a job to augment the family income became pressing. (still no London weighting). Me and Pete Morris got one as civvy cleaners at RAF Northolt; Not so far away and Pete had a car. The Americans were in one part and it was as if they had just risen from their desks and buggered off home. The English part of the place was bare with maybe a cardigan hanging over the back of a chair or a pair of shoes under one. We gave that up after a while. That's when I must have started down the Fox and Geese at Ickenham. It was about then we got a dog. Fatty Turner from next door was down the RSPCA and we thought it was a good idea and followed suit. Will we ever learn?

Jackie was looking pale and pasty, so down the docs who recommended we dose her up with Virol. A Cod Liver oil Malt mix. Take with spoon. I took another job at the Railway Arms in Uxbridge. Sat and Sun. First job bottle up. i.e. re stack the shelves. Hadn't been touched all week. Up and down the cellar steps. They did Karaoke weekends same old geezer on the piano and the same people groaning out the same songs wildly out of tune. It was dreadful. All that for a pound a night. I just stopped going. Moved round to the Metropolitan opposite the nick. Small pub old couple running it. Main business was weekends when there was a dance at Burtons, a step away. The place would be heaving for an hour. All under age but it was their best time of the week. There was a punch-up one night and the landlady sent me over the nick to fetch a policeman. I thought he'll end up nicking you. I gave that up too.

I'm down the Royal Oak Cowley for a drink. Big old fashioned pub. Lounge bar, off sales, public bar. John Roberts the landlord offered me a job. Azzaro was already working there. Civilised place, quiet conversation in the lounge with soft piped music. Food at lunchtime. Public bar with Darts, Cribbage and Domino's going all the time. Postman Pat was in the public bar every night with his sidekick alongside playing the odd shilling in the bandit. On Saturdays Rosie, Pat's wife would come and stand between them; have two Babychams and think she was having a good time. On a Sunday just before opening time. Pub all clean and shiny. John would be up at the window in the public and call out. Two pints of Bitter, two Mild, four Light and Bitters. At two minutes to, they'd be kicking the door. At three minutes past it looked like they'd been there all morning. Old Sid was a crib player and his wife Vera worked behind the bar. John Roberts said to me one day' She's robbing me, but I can't figure it out. You watch her. I already knew. Old Sid would pay his round with a pound note and she'd serve him and give him back a pound in change, then work the till to put it right. I was going down for a drink one lunchtime. Ah say John handing me a bunch of keys. What's this? My mini traveller. Pop over to the Brewery at Watford and get me a couple of kilns of Lager. The dray men are on strike but you can pick up at the brewery. John I'm here for a drink. I went to Watford.

When you changed a Whisky bottle it went over the dumb waiter. Quite a decent sized space. When it was fullish the bottles would be drained into a glass and poured into the Johnny Walker Black label in the lounge. In the cellar all the ullage from the drip trays would be poured into a sieve over an enamelled bucket. That went into the Double Diamond in the Lounge. John R. asked me to do his cellar: as in clean the pipes and fonts. Would take me three hours on a Friday afternoon. First bloke to do the job in spite of another's claims. I've mixed the chronology a bit here but no matter. After scrapping the Morris I acquired a Bedford Dormobile van from some where. It was dressed out as a caravan with curtains in the back. We had it for some time and people would borrow it for it's carrying capacity. The only drawback, it had no heater. Broke the windscreen. Disaster. Round to Bedfords. How much? £6. What a bugger. I'm telling Sally and she lent me the £6 bless her. When buying the same: a bloke in the spares place said don't forget the string. String? What was he on about? Once Alec and I started fitting the screen we realised the string was to help ease the rubber round the screen where it fitted. We managed. Not easy!

For a trip out we would go to Black Park at Denmead. Had a nice lake and some woods. We would also run down to see Nanny and Gramps. Bagshot, Oxshott and shitshott. handy because I could see my mum at the same time. her living at Emsworth. What happened to the van I can't remember. Possibly sold it to someone: because the last car we had before going to Malta was a Rover 90 which Dave Edwards gave me. The block was split after freezing. No antifreeze. I filled the split with Araldite. It was nearly a fingernail deep. Left it a week and repeated the exercise. That was a lovely car. Took us all including Mandy to Clacton one weekend. Some drive through London and out to the East coast. The Rover was supposed to be going to Ron Barrow. Joyce's husband. But the petrol pump was playing up and I never fixed it. Sod's law, the day I was supposed to drive it down to Leigh Park it expired and I left in Eastcote tube station car park.(no charges then). Told Azzaro who fixed it and flogged it. I never did get the money.

I went to Radio Rentals in Ruislip and asked for a job, part time, and they gave me one fixing telly's on my days off. Quite straightforward once you'd done a few. No! There wasn't a single housewife made any improper suggestions only one old queer living in Filey Way. I took Derek, Nicola's dad with me one Christmas. I think Derek was the best of the crowd that Heather shacked up with. It was probably then that Nicola fell off the swing.

Being a sergeant at last meant life in the mess and it was traditional to have a Battle of Britain Ball in September. Alec had a mate called Don who was sort of uncle to Mandy and absolutely doted on her. Nice bloke. Bachelor. Worked at Viznews for the BBC and I got him to make a tape of a wartime broadcast complete with sound effects. Azzaro and I approached Pinewood Studios out Iver way and borrowed some wartime props including the helicopter used in one of the Bond films. It was only a model but was used in the film. So we dotted them about the mess entrance for authenticity. Of course at the end of the evening some bugger had ripped the head off the sentry. We got it back but caused some embarrassment when returning the goods.

As I remember we were working in MT at the time helping the station. As it wasn't fully up and running we had to beg borrow and steal from other units. Not fully understanding the ethos of MT. Basically 'your get no wheels here pal'. And, not wanting the job and with the MT lads determined to do things their way. I often fell out with them. Mind you Norman Coyne took over and made it his personal fiefdom.

It was about now that Bill and Pat came to visit. They were off to Cyprus for a two year tour. Betty was well pleased to see them as she did enjoy a bit of company. Well it came to pass that Pat would rise early and bring me morning tea up. While Bet and Bill lay in for a bit. I was the only one working. We went over the families club one night all crushed in Bill's car. We'd taken someone else but I forget. On the way back after a decent drink, I had my arm round Pat to ease the room and found myself caressing her breast with no objection from the lady Once in the quarter, Pat and I went to make sandwiches leaving Bill and Betty in the front room. It was a long go frying the sausages and when we presented them Bill and Betty had retired. Bugger the sandwiches, Pat and I retired to the settee and made love. Unfortunate as Shakespeare said. Wine increases the desire but ruins the performance. Come the morn Pat brought up my tea as usual and once downstairs asked me what I wanted for breakfast and I picked her up and carried her through to the settee and finished the job. Then I went up and said farewell to Bill and it didn't hurt a bit. Tony Dennett said to me. What have you been up to Parker? Your like a cat that's been at the cream. Had a silly smile on your face all morning. I never let on!

We continued to party. Being in a group and living more or lass cheek by jowl 'twas easy. Had one at Sally and Alec's and built a screen loo for the fellas in the Garden. Girls only inside. Norman Coyne's wife Tyna made it obvious she was available. I won't say I wasn't tempted but living that close made it all too difficult, and should she have declared undying love and wanted to move in. We had nowhere to go and in spite of all Betty and my constant rowing I wasn't leaving my kids for a bit of nookie. Meanwhile Azzaro had got himself a job at Air Chefs at Sipson. He'd been in the King William P.H. and Air Chefs was next door. The job was catering Spanish night flights. (the costa holidays had taken off). They came in about half nine. One laid out the required number of trays for each flight and filled the Barketts with Grapefruit, laid open sandwiches from the kitchen on the plate along with cutlery. (not plastic). Placed all in the cabinets and loaded them on 'your' lorry. Making tea and coffee just before the off to the airport. John being John in the interim would take off in his lorry to find a pub somewhere returning in time for tea making. Until another task came along which was the Swissair strip. The Swiss air service landed about 8pm and the breakfast packed in Switzerland was to be refrigerated overnight before being reloaded in the morning. The booze cabinet sealed by customs was taken to the bonded store. John would leave the breakfast trolley on the back of the lorry for the morning man. It never did go in the fridge. And it wasn't long before he got me a job there. Bernie the supervisor. Got a driving licence? Show me. OK your in. There were no HGV type licences then. Late sixties. I soon learned the ropes. Had to go for an airfield pass. Photo taken printed and laminated all in ten minutes or so. I said to Archie the security man. You should get one and save the three weeks wait to get a West Drayton pass. One would drive out the airport and sit in the baggage handlers 'office' as they had a speaker from the tower. One would listen for one's aeroplane- i.e. 295 from Malaga being directed to gate. Echo 5 and if that was yours, off you go and open the back doors once it was parked and do the bizzo. The Spanish crew were very keen to get their milk which was on the invoice anyway; but if you played it a bit simple you'd be presented with two miniatures, and Ole! The milk appeared. We went on to supply, smoked salmon, cornflakes, cheese, and various other requests. Even got a cash and carry card. When John and I realised there was also work on a some Saturdays. One might be sent to a small aircraft to deliver a flask of Coffee, Take these Trifles round to the PanAm commissary on the other side of the airfield. Crumbs compared to Air chefs kitchen which was clean. Pan Am's was spotless. You could eat off the floor. I was sent over there once with twenty trifles. When I got there I had one big one. I learned to keep them in the lorry cab in future. As an aside: upstairs at Air chefs was a Mrs ??? who'd been wrapping Pan Am silver for twenty years. Talk about boring. On night shift the supervisor/watchman was Fat Barry. He was part of a gang smuggling cars out the country to eastern European countries. More on that later.

It was about now that John and I decided to visit Vic. Vic Azzaro, ex rear gunner Pathfinders, ex, Flt Lt. Ground Control Approach calibration flight had taken the Kings Head in Holt, Norfolk. He wanted John to familiarise the place so he could have a holiday. I asked Bernie if I could work Saturday to pay for the trip I clocked in to Air Chefs about eightish and the supervisor had to sign my card as the clock had stopped at 07:20 and I spent the day on odds and sods. John came in for the evening shift and clocked on. It's broke I say you'll need the supervisor to sign it. Looks O.K. to me said John. He was right. They paid him for the full day.

So, it was off to Norfolk in the Dormobile and finding the pub in the dark. One went in through an arch into where they stabled the horses. Nice town, a bit quaint with all these bucolic locals. The last landlord had been a captain in the Army and insisted being called captain. Suppose we're to call you Flt Lt they say. No! My name's Vic. Call me that. Vic was a card, full of droll sayings and views on life. He was sergeant aircrew at RAF Uxbridge, but they wanted him in the officers mess for his wit and company and simply ordered him across. He went on to become a bookie in North Walsham. He'd go round the pubs collecting bets. He eventually died there. It was a privilege to meet him and to have read his log book. We had a great weekend, sightseeing, boozing and generally living it up. I'd earned £25 for a weeks work at Airchefs and had to borrow £4 off John for my petrol money back.

The people that 'service' the airport airside. Cleaners, honey cart drivers, baggage handlers, caterers, bringer of steps ad infinitum. Well a new company was formed called General Aviation Services. G.A.S. This was an American company and the 'bruvvers' (unions) didn't like it. Weren't having it in fact. There was hell to pay. All out bruvvers. The executive are meeting. Well the unions won the day and the company left the airport and things returned to normal. Marriott the hotel people built a kitchen at Feltham on the other side of the airport and because the Air chef partners had fallen out the contracts man took the business across with him to Marriott. And most of the staff from Airchefs went too. Including yours truly and John. Same job, same Spanish night flights, same baggage handlers. One snag, Marriott had brought American lorries over. All Green and Chrome LHD. Said he couldn't buy British one's in time. I was working one weekend and was asked to go across to terminal three and collect Mr. Marriott luggage and deliver it to the Dorchester Park Lane. Actually I was the only bloke that knew where Park Lane was. So I was elected. Can you imagine trying that today? Thus when we loaded and drove over to the baggage handlers shop to await the aircraft 'gate' number, a very jaundiced eye was passed over the lorries. What's that then? My lorry. we work for them now. Same people same job different lorry. Their American. We're not having that . The bruvvers will be in touch with the union and we'll let you know. Oh come on Sid it's no different-FROST. They didn't exclude us from the place but they weren't happy. So come the executive to Marriott kitchen for meetings with the management. Management was only Mr. Stiller. Everyone held their breath. Up went trays of sandwiches and buckets of ice over several hours and eventually they drove away. Marriott was to be allowed to operate on the airfield. What a monumental bloody cheek! But then the Unions were all powerful. It took Mrs Thatcher and the miners strike to finally break their grip on power.

John and I said to Mr. Stiller that we needed some beer on the wagons as the airlines occasionally wanted some. He said next time in a wide American drawl. Hey boys I've put some beer on the wagons but I ketch yew drinking ma beer I'll get the air-force to hang you! We drank his beer anyway. Coming out of the tunnel at Heathrow one night and I was too close to the kerb. The rear wheels were pushed out by the kerb itself and the ladder on the side of the lorry hit a Vauxhall Viva alongside it. Had some young lads in it. We stopped and exchanged details and I left a note for the day shift. I never heard anymore. The chef Kevin would drive a lorry round the yard for the fun of it. He was trying to muscle in on fat Barry's car smuggling business. They met out on the Sipson road and when fat Barry refused he shot Barry dead. Yes they caught up with him. Locked up!

Meanwhile back at Ruislip Janine was still crawling over to Sally's. I think she spent more time over there than in ours. Shortly after all this excitement: John said to me. Put our notices in I've got us a better job. Job doing what? Builders labourers he say. Pays more money. So I worked a weeks notice and John didn't. Bit like when Harry met Sally. John done his drinking the Royal Oak at Cowley in the lounge where you meet a better class of drinker. One being Harry James a consulting Civil Engineer who liked to keep his hand in by doing a bit of casual work at weekends and needed some likely lads to assist with the humping and dumping. Harry would pick us up and we might detour to a builders merchants before heading off to Chalfont St. Giles. Mr Good the top man for Hoover had a house up against a hill and was convinced there was a room that wasn't included in the home. He'd got Harry in and the measurements showed there was indeed an empty corner of the place. So Harry was to open it up and convert it to a liveable space. So we laboured Sat and Sun and our hands bled and we were knackered. Harry say meet you in the Oak and I'll pay you. We met, he paid, we had a pint and went home to bed, Finished. Of course we hardened up and could do the work and have a pint or two. Must have worked for Harry nearly a twelve-month. Then the RAF decided that wasn't working due to contractor delays and some of us would have to go. Tony Dennett said to me why not put in for an overseas posting? Me? I'd never get it. Do it say Tony. Thus we filled in the request for overseas posting and bloody well got it. Malta. Knowing there was a chance of getting a duty free car in Malta I went to Lloyds bank in Ickenham and opened up a deposit account. I never told a soul. The last quarters we'd had I send Betty and the kids off to grandmothers a week or so in advance so I could really clean the quarter up for 'march-out'. Not possible at Ruislip. So come the day of the 'march-out', the place was far from ready, and, after an embarrassing morning with the barrack warden and the families officer I had to report to stores at RAF Northolt to assess the damages. The damages came to £145. I had in my secret account £145.

I was livid. Not just the embarrassment of sitting there, while they did the sums while looking with at this poor bugger who couldn't keep a quarter clean. And worst of all the opportunity to get a new car gone! Betty simply didn't understand and wouldn't change her ways for anyone let alone me. I wouldn't mind but talking to my boss Sqn Ldr Healy about unprepared quarters in the families club the night before. More embarrassment. I paid her debts off again with the debt collectors. Sally at the final farewell said how much she felt Betty had let me down, and she wasn't talking about the Quarter. I had a farewell drink in the Oak. John Roberts decided that as an ex seaman Rum was my tipple and proceeded to lavish them upon me and Maureen his wife put on a nice buffet gratis. Well pleased and well pissed.

So down to RAF Brize Norton and overnight in the RAF 'Hotel'. Which wasn't bad. Next day a flight in a Britannia of Transport Command to Malta. We arrived in the pm. and were transferred to a 'hotel' in Kalafrana.

MALTA G.C.

Or RAF Malta as it was referred to. We were given an induction to the Island and info re schools, hospitals, car purchase, police and the sloppy driving habits of the islanders. That one started out. When you have your first car crash. And some do's and don't's Very thorough. One could buy a duty free car in the first three months and keep it throughout or buy in the last three months and take it home. Day two and we were bussed round the Island looking at RAF approved hirings or rentals. Then back to the hotel at Kalafrana to 'bid' for the places we'd seen. The system worked on the man with the most points getting first refusal Me still smarting over Ruislip went for a more modest basement flat in Paola. Betty organised Jackie and Colin into schools, being Tal Handaq and Luqa and I went to work. OK for me again but enough this time to keep Betty amused and interested. The locals were friendly and there was always the families office. There was a round robin RAF bus to take us to work. Met Dave Godfray whom I knew from Buchan He simply said hello and told me a joke.

I was newly promoted sergeant everyone was expecting a corporal. W.O. Housby welcomed me and said you'll be replacing Sgt Martin when he goes. Not me sir. I come out as a civilian. Not been in this man's air force for years. I didn't want the responsibility. Been away too long! No choice, your the man. RAF Madelena was an old coastal artillery fort, converted into a Radar Station. Three heads, two display suites and a processing room called the 'radar office'. We were about a dozen tech plus the operations staff whom we looked after but didn't really mix. Lovely little place, canteen of course. Everyone had been there long enough and were well established. No hail fellow well met, come and meet the wife and kids. A junior technician name of John Goodeve suggested a weekly meet to try the local watering holes. Called creeping round the boss, but I was glad of the offer and with no car, more than ready to accept. We did get invited to a party in Paola and I said to Betty we get to join the community at last. Don't be daft it's a wife swapping do. We're not going.

I was having problems being back in uniform and went to see the doc. Sqn Ldr. Immaculate in his K.D. Sat behind his desk. china cup of tea to the fore. Listened to me and suggested I try some sport. He was never going to lay a finger on me in examination. I went a week later and asked to see the Wing Commander doc. Roly poly man, fag on. Let's have a look at you. Bags of reassurance. came away feeling superb.

On the technical side of things I seem to find myself working with a different somebody on a problem and having fixed the bloody thing was finally accepted as a member of the place. Bill Martin left. He was driving home. Syracuse by ferry and then amble through Europe as a holiday. Great Sgt ??? came and I said to W.O. Housby he's senior to me so he can be in charge. Housby said to me. It's an appointment, your in charge of servicing. End it! So we settled in and then came an opportunity to move. We'd lent the Army one of our 'married quarters and wanted one of theirs in return. I was the most senior to apply and we moved to a nice location in a block of flats in Ta-Xbiex. Top floor. I looked at cars. A duty free

Volkswagen Beetle was £630 would you believe it? I managed to scrape up the deposit and we bought a nice blue one. I parked it outside the flats and some Malt coming round the corner left a dent in the nearside wing. But we had wheels. I was still smarting from quarter damages and would go round to Charlie's bar in Gzeria Circus. Sometimes not coming home till late. It didn't help matters I know and eventually Betty took herself and the children off to the Red Cross. I found out where they were and after some soul searching we all came back to the flat.

W.O. Housby called me in his office one morning and asked if I'd be pallbearer. His brother out on holiday had passed away Me and five others. Marty Baldwin of Buchan fame arrived with Ellie and the twins in tow. They were in the next block. Most of the technicians had been made up now and were all sergeants. I'd come to terms with being I/c servicing. One of Marty's twins fell sick and was hospitalised and while there died. She's been sick while on her back and blocked her throat. Poor little mite. No nurse on watch. So that was another funeral.

The Royal Artillery were on site about Spring when the light was ideal and were testing shells of different shapes using a T83 Bloodhound missile radar to track the shells and their behaviour. Seems Nelsons round shot was the best. Ho Hum! I'd been asked if I wanted to join the sailing club and I jumped at the chance. The club had some Albacores, a Swordfish and a Wayfarer or two. Training on two days if I remember. Racing on Saturdays. Only sometimes the racing would get delayed so race on Wednesdays and sod the training. Eventually I got the hang of it and they gave me a Swordfish. Geoff took me out as crewman for the trip to Sliema creek where we had a regatta against the Army On the return voyage as we were entering our bay Marxasloxx that during a gybe as it is known that the boat capsizised. I found myself in the upturned boat, under water (me) and unable to get out. I really was stuck. I'd just reached the point where my diaphragm was spontaneously determined I'd breathe when I realised that a mast Stay was under the neck of my lifejacket preventing my escape. I had the wit to lift myself away from the Stay and surfaced, and gulping air while Geoff who had been going frantic came round to me. We righted the boat and sailed back without the Jib as an International signal that we were in distress: which no one in the club took the slightest bit of notice. Too busy discussing their own successes. Once ashore I dried off and buggered off home. There was a note on the club wall. Hammond Innes looking for company on his yacht for a voyage to North Africa,

Me and John Goodeve the junior tech entered a rally. He chose me for my brains but we came a very poor last. However it prompted us to organise one for ourselves. More of a treasure hunt with drinky poos and prizes back at Madelena. Went very well except come tennish the unit commander said I'm off now. Close the bar. He went and the bar stayed open for a bit. But walls have ears.

We went out to Ta'kali airfield which was disused and gave Betty some driving lessons; 'twas a dead loss. She never had a clue bless her. Kalafrana was where we would go for swimming. It was a Brit service family area and very popular. Poor Jackie got very sunburned and we had to seek medical advice We had been told. But these things do happen. The weekend we might do the seaside in the form of bays. Paradise bay was down some very steep steps. Melliha bay was better. Other than that not a lot. And then things changed. Dom Mintoff was elected as Prime Minister and promptly wanted an increase in the rent we were paying to garrison the Island. If you think about it. Why did we need to garrison the Island? The row went on for some time and eventually Ted Heath our P.M. decided to pull the troops out. That involved taking all the equipment out and shipping it back to U.K. It also meant posting for us all and records came out to do the job on the spot as it were. For us radar types if you'd done less than a year then Cyprus was an option. Over a year U.K. Me and Jocky Lyons had done thirteen months and records were adamant. No Cyprus.

The whole thing was superbly organised even if it was largely a sham. We were packing up Madelena as a radar station. The navy were doing their bit and the Army likewise. HMS Bulwark was in Grand Harbour Valleta and the crew who had been the Sergeants Mess returned the favour, come on board families too! We finished up in one mess and enjoyed the hospitaly for an hour or so. We're waiting to leave and a sailor walked by in a towel and Betty went off with him and returned with a Teddy Bear. Favours? I've no idea. I needed a helicopter on site to lift one of the aerials and the Navy duly supplied. The other 'perk' was report to the Bulwark and they would give you a helicopter ride. We went all over the island and Gozo too. I loved it.

While packing up the stations we were also advised to pack our own goods and chattels. Boxes were delivered and once complete, inform the families office and you would be moved as a family to the Kalafrana hotel to await a flight to U.K. and onward transport to the quarter/ home address that you had chosen. In our case having nowhere to go it was The Oak Circle Church Lawford Nr Rugby. That is Betty and the kids. Not the fella's. Now we could work them without worrying for their families. Next was to go to accounts and get a loan to pay off ones hire purchase commitments. Take one,s car to the docks for onward ferry to the U.K. Now move into barracks and get on with the job. It was quite enjoyable and different. Victuals were sent up daily for us to cook. That went down like a lead balloon until George Powis the W.O. organised an on site chef.

We thought we were getting near the end when Keith Briggs the Flt Sgt would produce a key and open another

106

store. George Powis said if he's got any more tucked away I'll have his guts for garters. Maltese personnel who were uniformed in RAF Malta. i.e. Malta only. Well they lost their jobs and were organised into a hanger as gofers. To use the Maltese word for friend Spien became know as rent a spien.

ENSA the forces entertainment people sent out a show. When it racked up in our mess they closed the bar. To ensure a good audience, We had a contortionist, the Beverly Sisters and Harry Worth. Harry Worth a children's comedian. Pooh! Well he never told a smutty joke and he had us in stitches. What a funny man. Talking to his manager after. He said Harry was a bugger for his Whisky, and if walking down the street talking and suddenly found yourself alone. Check the nearest boozer. All in all a pleasant evening out. Thanks ENSA.

Now as a team we were adrift in barracks we decided to try drinking in each others watering holes. It never worked and Johnny Johnson who wife was Chinese suggested the Chinese nosh shop. So we went. Eight of us settled down on one table and ordered a beer each: when Michael Caine came in with another crowd and sat at the other table with a small crowd. They were making the film Pulp. We never acknowledged each other and we had a pleasant evening. One beer first course, one beer second course. Mr Caine appeared to be holding court at the other table and never stopped talking all night.

Then it became more serious. When not working we would go for dinner. Crumbs the meals the cooks produced. They did a superb job feeding everyone. It was then across to the camp stack for whatever film was on then across to the mess for drinks that were not only duty free, but at cost. No need to make a profit. We were leaving. There was a bus outside the mess one night that the Navy had sent over from Valletta for a games evening. We went an had a ball. Beat them with my party trick, getting them to make a jury mast knot quicker than me. Good fun!

At last we finished Madelena and I came out of there on the back of a lorry load of scrap. The Type 80 Radar was left standing. Vice Admiral Templeton-Cotterill who was in charge of operation Overchain was heard to have said that the man that takes that down will spend the rest of his career in the Tower. So he obviously knew that the whole exercise was a show of strength and we would return. We did! What a waste of money. And from the old girl that 'did' for us and no doubt others and all the local businesses that relied on the money pumped into the local economy; Lost. Bloody politicians.

BACK HOME

Finally having packed up our Radar and lost our cars and our families, albeit temporally and gradually dwindled down to less and less troops on the Island, it was our turn to go. A morning Britannia flight home. I'd got Brother Arthur to go to Southampton docks and collect my car. Taking it back to his place on Hayling Island. On arrival at Brize Norton I'd filled in the immigration card with much disgust and bitching to the immigration officer about such forms and my country; and looking at me as he tore it up. It's for migrants. Welcome home.

So round to Arthur's and collect the Beetle and off to find Church Lawford (no sat navs in '72) and the family.
There had been a massive accident on the motorway in Fog a couple of days earlier with many killed. One could almost feel the lost souls haunting the place. Church Lawford was finally located and Home sweet home. Well it was after a fashion being temporary. We were posted to RAF West Drayton, which was up and running as a proper RAF station and were allocated a quarter at RAF Uxbridge. Amazing exercise really. Operation Overchain relocated

troops, took care of their families, their cars and their hire purchase debts. Shipped home all the equipment on the Island to U.K. Photographed everything to show was left clean and tidy

We were now living at RAF Uxbridge and Betty was back at the usual round of sorting out schools for everyone and generally settling in. At least we had some experience of the area. Ted Heath was P.M. and the unions were striking and we were on a three day week.(to conserve energy) Aside from us coming to come to terms with Decimal currency, which had come in while in Malta. We were having elections about every three months until we got a government. Albeit a coalition. With David Steel siding with the government for a say in the running of the country. John and Gwen were in Cyprus and Alec and Sally were living in Ruislip Manor. Your darling Harold as P.M. had given us troops a huge pay rise hoping we'd keep voting for him. Consequently we were able to afford houses. Average semi then in Ruislip was £5K. Thus affordable. Alec was down at Oakhanger in Hampshire

We would collect Sally once a week and drive down there and have a drink in the mess with Alec. He took me up to the see the kit which was a satellite tracking system. All very hush hush. Then the drive back home with me stopping in Windsor Great Park for a pee on the Royal Oak. No we never got nicked for drink driving. Just lucky! Sally did ask if we would have Mandy (only daughter) as a guest so Sally could go down and stay with Alec. Mandy was at Catholic school in Long Lane. I didn't fancy the idea. I thought Mandy was a spoiled brat and didn't want the responsibility. Fortunately Sally accepted the answer without prejudice. I read in a magazine that Danny La Rue the female impersonator had taken the Swan at Goring. I mentioned this to Sally as she'd met him when he was just out the Royal navy. We went over there. Sal Alec, me and Betty. He, Danny at the pub was surrounded by fans and

Sally was a bit diffident. I broke in with an Excuse me Mr. Carrol. (real Name) and made way for Sally, clutching autograph book with his signature from when he was in digs at her mums and used to curl his wig there. He was well pleased and reminisced for a moment before adding a current signature to the book.

Out the blue Marty Baldwin and Ellie turned up with their surviving daughter. They were on their way to Southampton and a voyage to South Africa where Marty had taken a job. How they found me? I don't know. What you doing with the car then? He had his Renault 12 from Malta. I'm going to give it to the first person that's nice to me. Last I saw of him. Funny returning from the Oak one night and there's John and Gwen ex Cyprus. Meandered across Europe on completion of his tour and straight round to us.

Jackie was going to the Greenway school which had a tough reputation but was a good school. Colin we got into Abbotsfield being a boys school, we felt he'd be better off there and Janine was now at one in Buttercup Lane. Jackie said about now that she'd like to enter nursing. I think she was doing Girl Guides at the time.

Having been re-posted to West Drayton, there were still some old friends there from our time as well as a new lot posted in. They had also brought the school up from Locking as the kit taught was at West Drayton and nowhere else. Although tied in to the overall defence of the U.K. They asked me if I would return to Malta and help put back the kit we'd just taken out. Can the family stay in quarters? No! They'll have to move to a records office quarter like Church Lawford. Well sod that: get someone else. The family has had enough disturbance of late.

The Turks had finally had enough of the Greek Cypriots yelling for Enosis. Union with Greece. They weren't at war with the United Kingdom, but we had sovereign bases there and families which needed repatriation. Would I like to go and help with the evacuation? Again I say. No! find a single man and send him. I've had enough of being buggered about.

I'd gone back to the odd night or so in the Oak and weekends with Harry on the buildings. Old habits. But same needs. More money!

R.A,F. West Drayton was now a 'proper' station. The civilian contractors had gone and we were fully staffed by RAF personnel. They decided the school teaching Linesman would be as well off at West Drayton instead of RAF Locking. Would I like to be an instructor? I wasn't keen, but it was suggested that I was more qualified, having begun with Marconi on the kit. I reluctantly agreed. Move across and start putting the course together and you'll be off on a Tutorial Instruction Techniques course shortly. Records Office had other ideas and I received notice that I was posted to R.A.F. Bishops Court. Northern Ireland. The school tried to stop it but no go.

Shame, we'd taken up with Alec and Sally again. Were doing the odd bit of sea fishing. I even went as far as to try sailing again. It got one off on a Wednesday afternoon. I gone a few weeks and each time on arrival at said venue. There'd be a scramble for boats and I'd be appointed. Officer of the day. Set the course. Start them off and score the finish. Well the Sun shone and it was pleasant, so I made no fuss. Then the officer i/c the club Chas Trussler say to me. The club needs funds you know and you haven't paid your subs. Your right I say. I've never been on the water either. Everyone is so busy pot hunting I never get a look in. Oh he say, I never realised. I never went again. Alec was now at RAF Stanmore and we'd have the odd night over there with him. Some do's in our mess and I'd meet Norman and Tyna. She was still offering but usually it was more on the lines of, who's a scaredy cat?

So. What to do? It meant another records office quarter in some god forsaken spot.. Another upheaval for the family and schools etc. We'll apply to the local council for a council house. Stay put as it were. Hillingdon Borough Council said, don't be ridiculous. We give you one and the kids will want one when they grow up. However there is a government scheme to reduce the population of London by lending councils money cheaply to lend on as mortgages to people willing to move to expanding 'new towns'. Here's a list. Seemed a great idea. So I went along and saw my mate John Hannam where I went for all things Insurance etc. He advised me that I could afford £8K5 at most. So I had a starting point. Funny there was a road show at the local hotel, focussing on Milton Keynes and we went to that. All beautifully laid out. Mortgage advisors, estate agents, the whole schmeer. No problem sir, we'll sort you out. £10/£11K easy, no problemo. I didn't take the bait. Locally I could have bought a prefab in Uxbridge under the railway line for £K8. We needed to do some thinking. The decision was to drive North-eastward looking at properties so we could stay with brother Mick and wife Pat at West Raynham and come back a different route still looking.

1st stop Dunstable. Estate agents. Very pretty young thing. Yessir I have a one bedroomed Almshouse. Next stop Stoney Stratford Yes sir, sort you out. Come and look at this cottage. Do I have to buy it if I look? Yes we were that naive. One had to enter from the back through the neighbours garden, Bin that. Northampton next and a real possible end of terrace largish Victorian type place. Then we thought. Who wants to live in Northampton? On to Kings Lynn and the Fairstead. Looked possible. On into town for a bit of lunch, buying a local paper. Saw the Reffley which was still building. Went and looked and thought: just right. Need fifty pounds deposit. Got no money. Off to see Mick and Pat in their huge American bungalow at Sculthorpe, full of excitement and finish up borrowing fifty pounds off Mike. Back to Chas Hawkins clutching same. Another pretty young thing. You'll need a solicitor. Would you like me to arrange one? Suspicion. No I'll get my own. Big, big, mistake. So having decided it was back to Uxbridge and see the council to arrange the mortgage. That went OK. John Hannam sent me to a solicitor in Northwood. We then started to make arrangements for the move. Eddie Wick whom I knew had a moving business in Woking and was the choice and I would go up in the van with Eddie and the furniture. There wasn't a lot of it. But it was a start. Betty and the kids to follow on the train. I'd sold the Volks to get the money we would need. Had a big brown settee, my mum's old gas stove, some beds and a table and that was about it. Yes I'd lost my Mum.

Arthur appeared out the blue one Saturday when I was due in the Oak. Mum had died. She'd lived on her own at Emsworth. She'd taken up with Taffy while at sea, much to my disgust. Didn't sit well with me. Mum with another man? No thought for her needs. She'd been a widow for years. But they'd split up, hence the living alone. Family funeral in Havant and a drink afterwards. She was 67.

I then thought I'd sort out one bit of business and on the pretext that I was going to the Oak to work. I went over to Tyna Coynes. (Norman was in Glasgow). I stopped in the Fox and Geese for a bottle of wine and round to Tyna's. We had a ball. I was there three hours. Loved it! I shall return. Back to the quarter and I let a tyre down to simulate a puncture for the late return. Kids said next day. We pumped up the tyre dad. No puncture. Out the mouths of babes and innocents.

So that was me off to Northern Ireland. There was a lad at West Drayton who had been to N.I. and advised me to book and pay for a berth on the ferry. You could reserve one but they wouldn't necessarily hold it without payment. This I did. Asked the 'office' if there were any special instructions for the journey etc. in consideration as to where I was going. No they say Just be careful. Rail to Liverpool and ferry to Belfast. I got my berth. Disembarking with everyone else I looked to see if there was any obvious transport. People were climbing into minibuses and things, but nothing I could see. Eventually I went over to a movements man. They have a brass wheel on their arm. Bishops Court? I thought I saw it here he say. Probably gone now. (no-one had said I was coming). Who are you and showed him my I.D. Right he say, hang about and we'll get you a lift to Lisburn. H.Q. of the Army in N.I. Being allowed in wasn't easy but eventually I was sitting in the sergeants mess enjoying a cup of tea. It must have been Summer. July/Aug. Late afternoon a long haired type stuck his head in the door and said: you for Bishops Court? Yes. I ventured outside and saw this falling apart type of J4 minibus in lurid green . I later discovered this was a 'disguise' along with the long hair to prevent the service drivers becoming targets. We were stopped on route by an RUC road block but our RAF I.D. worked a treat and we were through. It must have been about four when I arrived in brilliant sunshine at the sgts mess and was allocated a room in the 'stables'. They were a line of rooms down a long corridor in the mess itself. Some of us were in married quarter blocks a bit further away. I settled in and started meeting people. Some I knew from before. Radar was quite a small world.

Bussing to work and reporting to eng-co-ord I was told I'd be taking over Test equipment from Norman. Little office, keep the test equipment repaired and calibrated. There were two sites. Well four if you count the newly built married patch. Domestic site. Killard Point with the type 80 Radar and what was the airfield at Bally Wooden Turkish with a type 84 and two Plessey height-finders. It was to turn out to be the best two years of my career. Due entirely to the personnel and the camaraderie, and the relaxed rules. We were virtually confined to camp. Bally

Hornan the village never had a pub. Downpatrick was some miles away and the local driving standards lethal.

BISHOPS COURT
motto Guard and Guide

Flt Sgt Pickering was the eng-co-ord boss. He was the 'man' at RAF Buchan when I was on heads. but was soon to go, and it was then. W.O. Jack Parker and Chief tech Dougie Ellis. There were two airman for general duties and a civilian, Hugh Lowery. The technical crew sat in the canteen unless there was servicing to do. I'd been there a month or so and I got a letter from the solicitor telling me that the property (Reffley). was, and had been ready for six weeks and the vendor was insisting of interest payments of X a day. Currently standing at Y. I was gob smacked! I arranged a bit of leave and hot-footed it to Uxbridge. Ringing the solicitors I was informed that Mr. Wheatly is no longer with us. I was round there pretty quick for an interview with the senior partner. We had a stand up row about the handling of a simple conveyance and the subsequent cost to me. I noticed that he had included his bill and asked if he felt that there was any danger that I might not pay. Pointed out that the government would meet all my legal expenses as I was serving in Northern Ireland.
We finally agreed on him giving me a receipt for the full amount so I could present it at pay accounts for repayment and for me giving him half the money and a post dated cheque for the rest. He then dashed off to Ealing to see the vendor (Taylor Woodrow) and complete. I was round to Hannam, Hatton, and Sully in high dudgeon and let them know in no uncertain terms what I thought of their so called solicitor. I was also of a mind being in receipt of the bill to cancel the second cheque! I should have listened to the young girl in Chas Hawkins.
At least we were now able to to make arrangements for

115

the move, and to hand over the quarter. This time I went back and spent a week cleaning and polishing it for a clear handover. Visiting Tyna Coyne for a bit more slap and tickle. The incoming corporal complained about the sheets or something and was told to wind it in smartish The place was perfect. We had a dog while we were there. Probably Janine's wish. My youngest daughter had a penchant for animals. We also had a washing machine with rubber tubes on fitted to the taps. A push on affair. Making use of the cheap night rate electricity we done the dhobi at night. I remember getting up for a pee one night and could hear this drumming noise and thought? That's the water from the split rubber drumming on the ceiling. Coming down in the morning to find quarter up to it's door sill in water. The poor bloody dog sat in her basket looking as forlorn as possible and water from the split rubber tubing still beating against the ceiling. A quick cold shower to turn it off and start throwing out the carpets and mopping out the water. My neighbour said to me. Been washing carpets then? Yes we do it every Spring. No. I never told the RAF either. Well no doubt there would have been a great fuss. Same on the West Ruislip patch. We had a chimney fire one night and I called the brigade. Don't ring your bell it's late. They came did the bizzo, drank a gallon of tea before disappearing back into the night. And we never said a dicky bird. Azzaro knew. He was there. We were off to Tony and Ann's wedding at Banwell the next day. I fancy we were in Coyne's Commer van he used to have' John Driving.

The set up at Bishops Court in N.I. was providing a back door watch of the U.K. radar cover also acted in a civilian role offering steers for aircraft crossing the Atlantic who may have needed it: as Ulster this is Trans Am ??? and need a steer for Düsseldorf. We were augmented from a security point of view by the RAF Regiment manning gates alongside the RAF police, of which there were more than double the number normally employed. We never went armed but weapons were available. One could only use when reading from the yellow card (instructions when and where to open fire). There was a policeman sitting in the toilet next to the bosses office playing with his pistol when he discharged it. The shock caused him to to pull the trigger a second time. How he got away without a scratch, heaven above knows. He didn't get away from punishment though.

For the most part the place was left alone as not being part of the security forces. The school bus was fired on however, so they removed the armed escorts that used to ride the buses and all was well. Of course our visits to the firing range were every couple of months instead of the two years or so that was the norm. They also used to hold dances in the NAAFI but after a bomb was placed outside said NAAFI the practise was dropped. The locals didn't want their womenfolk mixing with the filthy English. The locals also used the airfield as a racing circuit. Paddy Hopkirk. That facility was withdrawn post bomb. There was a chief Tech name of Gerry Woodhouse who was seeing a local woman up in Antrim. Strictly out of bounds. The husband found out and rang the C.O. and said if youse don't stop this I am going to bomb your station. No only was Gerry posted that day but my 'oppo Dougie Ellis was made to see him off the premises as it were. At least as far as Liverpool. Dougie was going on leave. Dougie was always going on leave.

Relaxed rules? There seemed to be more pubs on the site than anywhere. From the Sgt. mess point of view we were a couple of dozen or so SNCO's A third accompanied by their wives and kids in quarters, and the rest married unaccompanied. We had a Whist night on Wednesdays and a disco weekends. Johnny Johnson would show a film Fridays nights usually' A big night out for the wife. They would come in on Saturday evening. Hubby would slip them off his arm and go to the bar to talk football. But the wives were soon chatting with the married/single men. The rule was to sit at the tables in the bar in full view About nineish when the disco man put on the Carpenters one would invite a wife to dance. Hubby still talking football. And, one would furgle. The dances could get quite erotic, at least until hubby came to claim her. All harmless fun for the most part. Only one RAF Copper spoiled it having escorted Mrs Chick home. Husband on nights. Persuaded her to let him have a bit. Which she did and later told hubby. It was common knowledge anyway. A couple of honorary members whom were locals. Ivy Clements was the wife of one and she was huge. Les one of the Rock Ape SNCO's said you can grovel for smarty points, or a super grovel which would get you an Ivy medal, and they don't come any bigger than that. So we made the most of it!

DIVERSIONS

There was a boat that we used for sea fishing. Bit of a bugger getting it down into the water and back. Sometimes we could persuade the Rock Apes to meet us for a tow back; but because they wore disruptive pattern fatigues were mistaken for security forces. The fishing was good. From Basking Sharks to Mackerel Took the C.O. Winpey Warwick trawling for Pollack. He was into one and for his efforts tore the crotch of his trousers and there's the C.O. fighting this Pollack with his wedding tackle hanging free. Sometimes we'd try coarse fishing. Crumbs that was easy. The streams and ponds were well under fished. In those days '74 various Commands had fishing competitions. So we wangled a trip to the Strike Command fishing Match on the Welland nr Cranwell. I went along as marshall.

Usual mix up. I flew to Derby along with a.n. other and the Notts Forest football team. when Brian Clough was manager. We were meeting Delphinium. (chf tech Del Dawson) from the Potteries. He had the maggots. About a gallon of them. We were to over night at RAF Cranwell nr Sleaford Lincs. Often refereed to as Sleaford Tech. We were met at Sleaford by minibus and transferred to Cranwell. Who? What? Oh there's a note on the wall here. Your in transit in A block. A block was at least a mile away and we managed to trap the driver before he left. How about something to eat? Dunno, dinner is over and nobody left any instructions. Try the NAAFI. Cheers pal. Off we go and settle in A block. At least someone had made the beds. Right we'll try for the NAAFI. Delphinium was worried about his Maggots, It was the Summer of '76 and a roaster. So he damped down a pillow-case, knotted it and hung it out the window in the bathroom. Out we went; got fed and had a drink. We walked back to the accommodation only to find the maggots had escaped and were all over the bathroom floor. Pick em up took forever and so to bed. Another walk in the morning to the mess, dressed in scruff order for the day. Nobody said a word; as in; Oi! who are you? I'm enjoying a huge English breakfast when a smart dressed civilian came up and inquired. Are you the fishing party? Would you like a packed lunch? Anything is possible. Shame you didn't organise a late tea or sandwiches last night. Yes please for lunch. As marshal I simply sat on the river bank or chatted to the fishermen. Pleasant day. Who won? No idea.

Flight back next day. Aircraft type? De-Haviland Dove sir. Crumbs. Does it fly? Only at 6000 ft. So back to Bishops Court. We had films once a week courtesy of the RAF Police. Handsome sod whose name escapes me. Dougie Ellis was keen on Daisy Close's wife Maureen and complained to me that between me and Johnny Johnson (the policeman). We had all the wives gooey eyed between us and he wanted a share. It was only that we danced with them sat nights. Though there were a few liaisons made but never followed through.

We the angling club had a word about some sea fishing and went to Ardglass to meet a certain Malakey Crangle (you've got to believe it). We arranged for a trip out on his larger boat. Not wildly successful, but enjoyable none the less. No, we never bothered again. There was boozing in the Buff lodge and we would visit the NAAFI when there was a disco on. The Bay City Rollers were all the rage and one of the mess waiters had a son in the band: so I got him to get me scarf for my Jackie who was mad on them at the time. I also bought two Celtic silver rings for my girls. Probably lounging in a jewellery box somewhere.

LEAVE TRAVEL

Trips home and back. Pick up at mess by MT about 6pm for the run to Belfast Docks and the ferry to Liverpool. If you'd booked a berth and paid for it, so well and good. If only reserved you could find it given away to a cash customer. A look round the bar and one could identify the various services by their choice of mufti. The Army in particular favouring tweedy sports jackets; Lovat in colour. Once docked in Liverpool next morning and through security and to the railway station. Having a warrant I was only allowed to travel cross country. Liverpool, Birminghan, Ely, Kings Lynn. The word was if you had less than 48hrs you could travel via London. I did once' Every ticket inspector thought I was cheating but after giving me a hard time let me continue. It was a twenty-two hour journey.

Once or maybe twice a year you could fly On one trip I overindulged the night before and asking for tea was told. No tea, security risk. I'd arranged for Fred Cawte my one time chief to meet me at Terminal 1. The aircraft was late and here I am sprinting through terminal 1 when my way was blocked by two large men. The production of my

I.D. magically opened the doors. Fred was well inside the terminal. Being in uniform in those days also opened doors. That was me going to see my solicitor. Another flight across found me at Gatwick with enough money for a cup of tea or ten fags. The fags won. It was about now that I finally got my London weighting. Paid in arrears of course providing one had claimed for it!

They had another trick on the ferry. One would rack up at Liverpool for the return ferry. Berth booked and paid for and the Army who controlled the boarding would stand you aside. Ferry has it's quota of military personnel. There was me and an Army officer both peed off but made no difference. One would be bussed to Heysham and put on the ferry there. I wandered off and persuaded the ticket inspector at the bottom of the gangway that as I had a berth paid for I should be allowed aboard. I later met the officer in the bar. You too was all he said! The other Army trick was to appoint you orderly sergeant, so if there was any trouble on board you had to sort it out.

The vagaries of the system aside we were still enjoying the posting. I was on free messing and accommodation, Fifty pence a day, bullet money and a small sum for phone calls home. I needed every penny as the mortgage and bills didn't leave a lot left.

Maureen Close and I were getting close. No pun intended. Thus if we appeared at the NAAFI dance they would play Blanket on the Ground by Billy Jo Spears. Talking of music. Me and Maureen would take the quarter kids to the beach. Castle Ward a National Trust property. Maureen and David had a daughter Samantha, a welcome diversion when out: from the increasing desire to get in her knickers. Not that she wore any. Goodnes Maureen was a sexy woman. Being confined in a way to camp everyone in the mess was out to enjoy themselves and we decided to put on a show. A parody of the Generation Game. Bruce Forsyth's Saturday night at the Palladium. Half a dozen wives dressed in camouflage fatigues were put through their paces as new recruits by the resident weapons man Willy??? Me Dougie and Laurie Horner blacked up and cross dressed mimed the Three Degrees. Went down a treat. A mess waiter mimed a man on the underground. The 'piece de resistance' we opened the curtains to reveal a toilet pedestal complete with cistern. Daisy Close went among the Warrant Officers and brought them up on stage. One on the pedestal and the others earphones and music. Twenty questions for a hospital men's glass urinal engraved the messiest mind of the masters. Warrant Officers were also Masters. i.e. Master Pilot, technician etc. For the cuddly toy part we had people walking round in a ring. David Close (Daisy) did the quiz and the music. Joss White did the lights. Right first time from the crib Dougie gave him. Dougie produced it and we all had a lot of fun. It was intended to repeat the show in the NAAFI for the troops, but like all good intentions it never happened. I went for a drink afterwards but got fed-up being goosed as a Three Degree and went off and showered. The boss next day who knew nothing of the show asked me what I'd done to myself. Hugh Lowery pointed out that it looked like I was wearing make-up. I hadn't got the - paint, face, camouflage brown completely off.

It was Summer and the sun shone and there was the Amazons singing Mississippi, Demis Roussos, the Bellamy Brothers, Dr Hook and the background to the whole Summer was Mississippi and I was in Love. I'd now finished in test equipment and moved to Killard Point where we had a type 80 Decca Search Radar. Watch boss! Me, a junior technician or two if you were lucky. Had an airman arrived name of Parek. Showed him round the kit' Asked what he's done to get posted here. I applied for the east coast he said. Well this is the east coast. We were standing in the main equipment hall known as the radar office. I said I'm off to lunch. See you in half and hour.

Look after the place. When I got back he hadn't moved. Afternoon shifts ran from 1300hrs til 2100hrs and one cooked on site. The SNCO usually cooked, being a bit more experienced in the kitchen and the lads washed up. We also decided to have a Fete. Games were organised. Hoying the wellie, archery and the like. I was on tea duty. Big urn of tea. The C.O. (Wimpey Warrick) stopped for a cup. Tuppence a cup he asked? You'll not make a profit at tuppence a cup. Got it from the airmans mess for free. I might have guessed you old rogue. I'd now been promoted to Chief Technician and collected my GSM. Thirty days in the theatre being the qualifier. So I was well pleased with myself.

COURT MARTIAL

Strictly against the services own rules for accommodation. No two men rooms. Where did they live? Two man rooms.
Thus it came to pass that (alias) Tom was fellating his room mate Philip. Who had no business being in N.I. as he was under eighteen. He was whipped away and discharged. His crime being frowned upon in the service. Tom, currently in the nick at Aldergrove would be made an example of to deter others. Poor old Tom. He was quite popular and the grass roots feeling was: so what! Life's too short.
Once the full majesty of the law was assembled, Tom was released back to Bishops Court for the trial. He wasn't under close arrest and we all went over the Buff lodge and gave him a great piss-up!

IN COURT

All those wishing to attend the court will wear No1 dress and medals will be worn. There was the R.A.F. legal team (about three). A real Judge to keep within the bounds

123

of the law. I don't remember anyone representing Tom but someone must have I suppose. We come not to Laud Caesar but to bury him was the watchword of the court. The charges were read out in detail being more or less the same over several occasions. By number three or four Tom said he couldn't remember that one. Judge. You can make a defence of not remembering but you must not pretend you can't remember. Recess the court and phone calls to the legal department ad nauseum. Back in court and carry on. Guilty as charged. Nine months in the Glasshouse at Colchester and discharged with ignominy. The Bishop, the Bishop of Edinburgh no less had written to the court pleading in mitigation for mercy. Mercy? We decided before we came. We're going to hang the bastard as an example. Pour Encourage Les Autres. The thing was. The grass roots were all sympathy for Tom and nobody gave a toss about what he was accused off.

MISBEHAVING

It was the battle of Britain Ball in the mess and dancing with Maureen (Mo) and priapic as usual. and her without any knickers as usual. I'll come over to your quarter later that night with a six pack. Surprising David. This I did turning up about 2200hrs. Had a drink together and retired. David was on earlies next day and I was woken by Mo kissing me and once I'd cleaned my teeth, we were at it. Cor! I enjoyed that. She was some bunny. Dressing quickly and was leaving when David appeared having been suspicious and returned from work. Thinking all was well we took him to Castle Ward for a day out, with Mo and I canoodling in the background. We never got the chance again apart from runs to the beach with the married quarter kids. David finished up sick with a bad back probably over Mo and I. But time was up and I'd done my two years and was posted to Neatishead which I'd applied for. One was usually given ones choice after Northern Ireland. Betty came over towards the end. It was sort of tradition. The Flight Sgt had a spare bed in the old quarters. I'd managed to get her an indulgence flight from RAF Northolt. £12. typical Bet. 1st night in the bar and she wouldn't leave. In the end I left her to it. She found her way back to the quarter even though it was the first time.

So me Betty, Dougie and Daisy and Mo all squeezed into Daisy Close's big Sunbeam and did the tourist bit. Tollymore Park, Castle Ward, found ourselves in Crossmaglen and exited from there in a hurry. Saw Betty off at the docks at Belfast for the ferry and rail journey home. I spent the last afternoon up in Daisy Close's bedroom with him and Mo. Yes I had it bad. Trouble was I hung about too long and arriving at Aldergrove to find my aeroplane about a 100ft above the runway. Round to the guardroom and get a bed for the night. Sitting at the bar when I went in was Les, the chief rock ape. So we had a nice chat over a bevy.

EXIT N.I.

Off to movements next morning to see what was what, and they agreed to ask Northolt to fit another seat on the N.I. secretary's Hawker Siddley 125. Come back at 1400hrs. Which I did. My baggage was loaded and I was advised to sit in the first seat I came to on the left. Take off. Would sir like a drink? A G&T would do nicely ta! That followed by a snack and we were into Northolt, and I'm thinking. How am I going to get to the underground? Well there's the RAF all lined up as we deplanned at the salute. Black Austin 1800's awaiting and I'm stood there like a lemon wondering how I was going to get to Northolt tube station when the N.I. Secretary Merlyn Rees? asked if I had a lift. Replying in the negative, he said we can offer you a ride, we're going to the Home Office. Thank you very much sir and I climbed in the back while the chauffeuse took off at a rate of knots. He and her chatting about work before turning to me and asking. Who are you? Me? R.A.F. posted RAF Neatishead after two years service in N.I. When we arrived at the Home Office he say to me. Where next? Liverpool St Station. Oh! No problem, Angela will take you. And it was round to the station, toot suite. The train was virtually waiting and I got to Lynn early evening. fastest trip ever. About six hours as opposed to twenty.

Catching up with the family news. Jackie was about to start nursing. Colin was still struggling with his maths. Janine of course was still at school (when she wasn't playing truant) which is now Springwood High. Next problem was to get some wheels for the run to Neatishead. Bro Michael ran me to R.A.F. Coltishall where we were billeted as there was no accommodation at Neat. I checked in and got assigned a bed and Mike and I having asked were directed to The Goat P.H. where it seems they only kept opening hours. We only had a couple as Mike had to drive back.

R.A.F NEATISHEAD

Caelum Tuemur (We watch the sky)
Got the service bus in to Neatishead and made my number with eng-co-ord who sent me over to the 12 building and I was assigned to Test Equipment. Neat was a Master Radar Station with two search heads three height finders a high speed aerial, which never moved and the secondary Radars. Two buildings 11 and 12: engineering H.Q. and Station headquarters. Plus the 'hole'. As Buchan a below ground ops centre that was subject to arson by an airman. (subsequentially jailed) from which three firemen lost their lives tackling it!
The 12 housed the T85 Radar which was the most

126

powerful at 65plus megawatts. Mostly it ran at two or three. 'twas an AEI design. The Type 84 was a Marconi search head and the HF200's were built by Plessey. There were offices in the 12 and as EETEC. Electrical Engineering Test Equipment Co-ordinator sat in one. Harry Greenwood who I was with at Buchan was the incumbent. He was a bit short of the full shilling having been blown up in a Landrover whilst serving in Aden. (Radfan rebellion).

The R.A.F. had system where one held an inventory for the equipment one was responsible for. It was taxpayers money and someone had to take the can. It was only the inventory holder who could order parts. So me and Harry went off to the remote radio sites to count and identify his inventory., and to show me round as it were. On return late pm the Flt Sgt Cartwright, called Hoss after Dan Blocker in Ponderosa but was a totally different animal. He was an odious creature and was written up for promotion in glowing terms by his bosses, just so they could be rid of him!

I took over from Harry in test equipment and discovered that he ran the families club in Fifers lane near the married quarters and applied for his job there. Give me something to do in the evenings and a chance to meet everyone. Which I did. That went well enough and at chucking out times a man would come in with a basket of fish and have a drink while doing a bit of business. And, on occasion we'd retire to someone's quarter for some more. Sometimes I'd be invited to stay the night. Get the settee like. I'd be up in the morning and gone. I was getting advances from Mary. She was Bob Young s wife and Val Banner was coming on a bit strong. All a bit of fun and quite relaxed. Bob was our job co-ordinator. Quite a lot of co-ordinators in this man's Air force. He made sure all the routine servicing tasks were carried out and the job cards filled in and filed.

I finally managed to acquire a car. Got a Mini from the

Poplar Garage that was then in the Wootton Road where the Ski/windsurfing shop now is, or maybe was. Hoss Cartwright had arranged for me to take some visitors to Helicopters at Coltishall. I got a phone call from Dougie Ellis to say Mo and David were visiting and get myself up there (Beverly) smartish. I pointed out that it was quite foggy and it was too much of a risk. But he would brook no argument and I duly set off late afternoon. Took me three hours or so and although the Fog was thinner in Yorkshire, it was closing in fast. Once we'd said our hellos we went out for a drink at the local pub. Crumbs said Dougie it's quite foggy. We all had a decent evening. Doug complaining to me the next day that he'd dropped Mo a note suggesting a closer relationship and was well disgruntled that I'd beaten him to it. My letter from Mo! Poor old Doug. His wife was the church social type who wore hats with bunches of Cherries on. All very prim. He divorced her and within a month she'd married again. Just goes to show. I got away the next day but was delayed on route and had to ring Helicopters and make my excuses. I never wanted the job anyway.

Back to the families club. Christmas dance? New Years dance So I had little choice but to stay and run the bar with the corporal. Betty and the kids came and we stayed at Bob and Mary's. The arrangement being to exit the club at the end and return in the morning to wash-up and clean up. Betty and the kids doing a bit of shopping in Norwich. It was a bitterly cold night and Betty and I were sharing a single bed. I was sleeping in the raw as usual and needed a pee. Thought that's only a moment across the landing and off I went. On return as luck would have it, there's Mary coming up the stairs. I froze and then dashed into bed. A moment later Mary climbed in beside me. Another moment later a voice (Bet) said. Tell Mary to get out the bed. Bugger. Come the morn and I was off to clean the club up. Betty never went to town. To Bob's consternation Mary never surfaced until after I returned about Noon and taken all my lot off to town and then home. A difficult and embarrassing moment. Betty never made too much fuss about it but it raised her suspicions. Val Banner was another who had a fancy for me. Or was it scalp hunting? Val would come over the club and do a spell behind the bar. I was out with Johnny Biggin an operator whom I got on well with and on return to the club to lock up, Val reminded me we had a date. So locking up the club saw me round her place for a bit of nookie. I wouldn't mind and it had been snowing and there were two sets of footprints leading to the door. What will hubby say in the morning? Not to worry she say we have an open marriage. It wasn't much later that Mary wanted to meet me and we'd go off and have a jar followed by a hotel. Having agreed and on second thoughts decided it was all getting out of hand and I let her down. Typically we had another Kipper sandwich night and Bob Young insisted I stay the night. Another settee. Come the morn Bob had caught the bus to work and Mary got to work on me. I think she saw me as a way out of her marriage. Getting to work late I asked Bob why he never woke me, or waited for a lift in? He was evasive but I got the impression that he knew what might happen and was happy with it.

MORE EDUCATION

I got shifted again. Selected for the control room course. Watch Boss. The status of the type 85 Radar was displayed on a mimic. 3000 or so tiles forming an eight foot display showing the status of all the transmitter and receiver equipment. Likewise the other Radars. To hand, telephones, tannoy, radios. On was king of all one surveyed. Once you'd learned the bloody thing. Thus the need for a course. At Locking as usual. Three months I think. There were four of us. Ian Moreland. Sid, Tom

Tucker, who was with me at Madelena. and a Sgt (unusual) it was normally a Chiefs job. They were short of accommodation and I was put in a four man room. Fortunately the only occupant. The course wasn't arduous and being SNCO's there were no station duties. Trouble being shortage of money. Servicing Reffley was a months salary and Betty could go through money and have absolutely nothing to show for it. Me and Ian Moreland signed out some golf clubs from the sports store and played pitch and putt round the officers mess from Monday thru Wednesday, only allowing one night in the bar. We didn't get away too many weekends either. One bloke used to drive up to Alnwick each weekend. So it was time for a site visit and some practical. Neatishead being chosen and accommodation arranged at the Recruiting Sergeant in Coltishall village. I rang the man and cancelled as I would be at home. Seems the others found other things to do and the landlord of the Recruiting Sergeant complained to the RAF. Our course boss and ex ranker was hopping mad and insisted we all write a grovelling letter to said landlord but the Easter weekend early get away for us was cancelled. I wasn't having that crap. so excusing myself to the class instructor, John Facey went along to the bosses office and knowing he was an ex corporal told him he couldn't award punishment without a charge being made. He backed down and the 3pm getaway was restored.

Bill Ranson was an instructor now and renting a room with Mrs Roberts where he stayed before. Only he was single now having divorced Pat for extra curricular activities in Cyprus. Like a lot of men he was in to sport and his hobbies leaving a bored wife at a loose end. The Devil makes work for idle hands. He had a girlfriend Liz. Bill's weekend routine was to take his dhobi round the laundrette and drop the woman to do it for him. Round the pub for some pool, back for the dhobi and a carry out for lunch. Pub at night. Sundays down to Fanny's which hosted a Jazz Band. The place was standing room only and one's feet stuck to the carpet. Who cares. Great music. Then at a fun run he met another Liz. Something clicked and he dumped the first Liz for this one. I met the first Liz down the pub one night and started staying round her place. It was standard practise with most lads coming down to Locking to make a bee-line for the nurses home to fix themselves up for the duration. I never did as a rule but let the rule go hang this time. That was the Queen's Jubilee year and Betty and I were drifting apart at a rate of knots.

All were safely settled in on the Reffley and it was quite a nice neighbourly place then with bottle parties. Jackie had started nursing training at the QEH. I met some of her classmates and they seemed great gals. Ruth, Frizzbonce. Colin was still struggling at school and having got assaulted at the swimming baths I had the police call me at work and asked if I would prosecute. They would do the bizzo. I was also in court another time, where Colin and his mates had attacked a lamp-post. That was a twenty-five pound fine. I seem to remember the council gardener and the other bloke paid up and I needed time to pay. Oh and Janine was probably still bunking off school. I'd taken her Blackberrying up Nursery lane and discovered the Swan P.H. Was a Sunday lunchtime and I walked into a busy pub and almost at once Bill Green said. Yes my friend. Couple of packets of fags please. I thought I've just found a decent local. Derek in the New Inn was liable to look at you and walk away. Service there was non-existent. Betty was working in Limberts fish and chip shop cafe in Norfolk Street, waitressing. If I was off, Janine and I would run up there on a Saturday evening to pick her up and rush back for Buck Rogers in the 25 century.

SHIFT BOSS

I was put in double harness with Chalky White, a

retiring Chief. He was a bit of a martinet, ran a taught ship. One had upwards of a dozen men to control. The Type 85 radar was a continuous job for two men Type 84 a technician for that and two men doubling as fire watch. Three height finders,secondary radar, display and processing equipment. The high speed aerial: couple of mechanical guys, some erks for gash jobs and the canteen to run. A super-tech sgt, me and an officer. back to Chalky White. I've seen him in the rest room watching telly while the lads were running around cleaning the place. Oh! Chief, so and so's on the telly. Tough I'm watching the news. He had a board with everyone's name on it and on pain of death one had to come in the control room and tick the box of where they were. There was even a box for the loo!

So Chalky went and I settled in to the job under an Officer. His job was to sign leave passes. Administer punishment and report to the sqn commander. However he could read and run the control room. It was four twelve hour days followed by four twelve hour nights, and four days off. We had a tannoy to summon people and or other messages. All the radar returns were piped to the local displays and down to West Drayton. Thus all the radar coverage in the UK was available at West Drayton. Overall boss was a Wing Commander with the 'wing' being divided into two squadrons: one with an American exchange officer a Major who's office was in the 12 with us. Once Chalky had departed leaving me in charge I asked one of the corporals Bill Smith to cut the board down just leave room for peoples names and their assigned task. i.e. helping the station defence officer, driver etc. I'm sitting there king of all I survey and I needed a technician to investigate a fault that was highlighted. There was no response to my summons. Nada. They were all at dinner. Didn't I feel a damn fool. I considered my position. Come the evening I left the boss in charge and called the troops into the rest room and dished out my first watch bollocking. How I wanted it or it would be back to Chalkies rules. This became a regular tool of mine when I felt they were slacking off. It worked. As a counterpoint I take them down the pub at end shift sometimes so they could poke me in the chest and get it off theirs.

So I had wheels and settled in to the routine of the job when somebody called a Taceval. Tactical Evaluation of the Units ability to defend itself. What a bloody pain that turned out to be. The official team of examiners would turn up unannounced and we'd all be running around like blue arsed flies trying to defend the station against attacking Rock Apes while carrying out normal operations. They usually lasted five days. The subject to the assessment got the C.O. promoted. So then we practised min-vals. C.O. type vals. New adjutant arrived we need to show him how we do it. We'd done most of our shift with one night left to do. My shift had spent the weekend erecting tents. No! Ops always wriggled out of these things. Tents? Yes it was a lock-in while we did the business plus the Nuclear phase. The engineering Warrant Office arranged for the bar to be open at end of day shift. I suggested that it stayed open in the morning for the end of night shift. Don't be ridiculous!

To rub salt in the wounds the day it was finishing the last phase to do and my lads had gone to bed and lo! They were opening the gates and letting the Ops out. I got on to my boss, the Winco and told him in no uncertain words that my shift had been there for ten days already and they were beginning to smell, so they were going home for a decent bath and bed before returning for the night shift. Yes Chief he say. They told me when I got to the Oman that the Taceval had been abandoned. Commanding officers having better things to do. So it all settled down and I'd go off to Neatishead for my shift. Me, Fred Head my sgt. whom I got on well with. We lived in the Sgts mess at RAF Coltishall and we'd take it in turns to drive in. He was

Michael really but was dubbed Fred and it stuck.

We maintained the Radars, bollocked the troops from time to time. Played silly bloody war games to distraction. The running of the canteen gave us an income from the sale of tea and coffee. The Crisps, chocky bars etc were provided by me all properly audited and accounted for. On the fourth day of the shift I'd suggest we all repair to the Swan at Horning for a bit of team building. Said to J/T Patchett i/c watch slush fund. How much in the kitty Dick? Er nothing chief, just an i.o.u. in there from me. Strictly a severe punishment but we all liked Dick so it was ignored. The American Major asked me for a driver one night for a lift home. I said you can have J/T Patchett. O.K. Great chief. Ah there you are Dick. Major it's Junior Technician. Yes Chief: come along Dick let's be out of here.

I enjoyed being in charge of a shift. I'd got the hang of it and was a bit of a martinet, but I was the one reporting to O.C. Eng of what was and what wasn't and why. Back to war games and I was usually guard commander even if the set up said I should be on engineering. The engineering officer came to me on one exercise, he'd been out checking on remote radio sites. He said there was a couple of cars parked at the end of the lane and they were still there when I came back. They're probably a courting couple, but I want you to check. Out we went and I suspect it was a married man and his paramour. We had no authority outside of camp but I stopped and approached them. I said, we are playing war games and we detected you on our instruments (load of old guff that) and are checking to see if you are genuine. They retired to their own vehicles and were gone. Probably thought we could overhear them. I trust we didn't break up that romance.

Then it snowed. The roads around the site being up to four feet below the fields soon filled up. I was living in this cottage about half a mile from the site and being on night shift made my way in via the fields. Then I came across people with spades digging. Where did you spring from? I said. What are you doing? We're digging out the C.O.s car. I went on in. I'd no fags and was gasping. Straight to the canteen and get a packet. Heaven. Ah! Chief say the officer, we need to dig our way out. I want you to organise relays of troops to do so. Negative on that Sir. You will only exhaust the men. Our job is to maintain this Radar Station. We have power, food and water. Should we be here for days Coltishall can helicopter in supplies. I still want the site roadways kept clear. Right I said but I want Rum for the troops. I'll ask the Medical Officer. Do it! It's in the regulations. The officers mess sent over two bottles and later in the week we got an Anker of the stuff, The troops loved it. I was No.1 with them! Coltishall M.T. eventually cleared the way through and I even managed to persuade them to do the lane as far as my cottage. As I said I was quite happy running the shift. I had two good sgts for taking over and ensuring all was well. There was a shortage of engineering officers and I was mumero uno! A hard working bunch of lads, for the most part. Right lads outside, trailer pump drill! Oh Chief. It's Tiswas. Tiswas? What's that?. A Noel Edmonds programme on Saturday mornings for kids. Out! Trailer Pump.

An aside for the moment. Brother Michael who had been working at Ross foods Fakenham after leaving the RAF on redundancy decided he needed to go to Saudi Arabia with BAe. He said he had some MFI type furniture coming and would I go round and mantle it up. Bit of a pig like all those flat packs. But we managed. Then one night Betty received a phone call from Pat asking to borrow me. One of the barmen in the Crown Hotel Fakenham where she worked as a barmaid wanted to show her his new flat and she didn't want to go alone. Betty was all for it, and as it happened I was due to start shift next day and was shuffled off to the Crown. At pub close it was round to the blokes flat for a looksee. I wouldn't mind but he was as queer as a nine bob note. I was more at risk than Pat. So round to Chusan and drop Pat off. She say to me come in for a coffee and then bed. Seemed like a good idea to me at the time, even if I did fancy it was a set up from the start. Became a bit of a routine. Me off to start shift the night before and overnighting at Chusan. Not a nice thing to Cuckold one's brother. But it's a strong aphrodisiac.

The Queen's cousin was visiting to inspect the station and a visit plan was drawn up. The itinerary of where everyone would be. Who was to open doors, who would have umbrellas in case of rain. Even ensuring he would be addressed as Your Royal Highness. I said to my boss. I'm on duty that day and I'm not mentioned. No he say. We thought we'd hide you away for the control room part. Was I that rough a diamond?

Then disaster. I was posted to RAF Boulmer. I only had a couple of years left to do. I rang records and spoke to Terry who was responsible for our postings. He say there's been a promotion at Boulmer and somebody has to go and you've been there the longest. No I say. How about Eric Harding the day chief? He's been here that long he's bought a house in Potter Heigham and his kids have all done their schooling there. No say Terry he's only just returned as failed officer trainee and is considered 'new'. Well, Roy Venton. He's been here forever. No say Terry it's you. But I have a house in Kings Lynn. I know he say but if you like I'll make it a detachment. Six months. What pissed me off was that we'd just had four chiefs visit for their control room practical. And records bloody well knew that there was a chief at Boulmer due for promotion. Could have used one of them. No Parker your the chosen one.

R.A.F. BOULMER

It's 1980 and I'm up there: same same Neatishead. The boss welcomed me and said I'd be doing leave relief. So it wasn't even a proper job. Four days as sergeant on that shift then twelve as chief on another And a Tacevel due! To add insult to injury Terry had made the detachment five and a half months, which meant I couldn't claim disturbance allowance or sod all else that six months would have allowed me. I told the boss in no uncertain terms what I felt about it. No choice but to buckle down to it.

Alnwick is a lovely place and Alnmouth even nicer: but I wanted my job back. A five hour run from home in the old Morris 1800. I sweated it out and when it came time to go the boss said to me; you arrived here bitching like a pie-ard, but shut up and got on with it. Thank-you!

NEATISHEAD (AGAIN)

Well in the six months gone things had changed and they really didn't know what to do with me. I'd lost my shift. They stuck me in an office and gave me odd jobs to do. Canteen manager. Paper pusher. Talk about having one's legs cut off at the knee. The engineering boss then was a Wing Commander Peberdy. He came to me one evening and said. Take this shift over now. The one currently working. I've sacked Chief John. (forget his name even though he was at Bishops Court). I don't think Peberdy had told him as he was nonplussed. I said to John you may as well bugger off now. I don't finish until 20.00hrs he say. Well your out of a job so sod off! The wing-co rang me later. In the dark on his motorbike Chief John had been killed in a motor accident outside Coltishall. Don't tell the shift. I felt they should know and called them in to the control room and informed them. I felt rather guilty for suggesting he went home. Such is fate. The wing-co came in to tell the troops but I had beaten him to it. A Flt. Lt. Bagley was immediately appointed family liaison officer. To inform the family and to offer such assistance as the service would allow including a military funeral if they should wish. I ran on with the shift but my old 'friends' had gone and my heart wasn't in it anymore. So our time was coming up for discharge and I never applied to sign on for age 55. Even though I might have made Warrant Officer. If I went at forty-two then I had a chance of getting a job. At fifty-five? Doubtful. A life choice. They dined me out as the custom was and presented me with a decanter and six glasses; all engraved and all broke now. On my final day I simply walked out the gate and drove home. What an anti-climax.

I'd applied for a place on the fifteen metre yacht Lord Trenchard that the RAF had, to give us a taste for sailing. It was the turn of Neatishead. I was accepted and went down to HMS Hornet in Gosport to join. Sqn Ldr Adam Wise equerry to one of the princes was skipper. Flt Lt Colin Bagley first mate and we were six more on for fun. Discipline was now for the needs of the yacht and relaxed. Sitting in the cabin and one of the youngsters lit up a fag. Adam Wise said to him. If you do that you'll never make forty. Quick as a flash he replied. Nobody's effing forty. It was quite amusing at the time. We were advised to stay close to the English coast because of bad weather forecast in the channel. For the first day we were shown the ship and what was what and where and how to use it. We sailed from Hornet and stooged round the Isle of Wight, learning to make sail, change sail, steer and cook on the ridiculous stove the thing carried. Fortunately we carried field rations which were easy to heat and eat.

Day three and Adam thought we should run for Le Harve and bugger the weather. We did getting there late evening in the dark. A quick run ashore for a drink and a sandwich. I don't remember whether we spent another day there but the run back was at night and I'd volunteered to cook the supper. Once I rolled aboard late and full of beer I missed it. It was a wild night and a straight run to the Needles where we tucked ourselves in and anchored for the rest of the night. The next day we wandered back to HMS Hornet to cleaned the ship up and hand it back. Getting wet had given me a humdinger of a Cold, so it was straight round the Chemist for a boat load of remedies. I have a memory of sitting in a pub in Gosport with Betty, Janine, and a.n. other when a couple of sailors in uniform stopped on the way out and each stole a kiss from Janine. I was amused. Janine was quite pleased and surprised.

There were plenty of courses available from a day to a couple of weeks to help one rehabilitate into civilian life. I did a couple of day courses and a fortnight at Danbury Park in Essex on small business ownership and management. Quite enjoyable learning bookkeeping and simple accountancy. They had people visit and tell their experiences. Gave one an insight into some ideas for oneself. I fancied either a franchise or an ironmongers somewhere. I even gave the Post Office a thought. I should have passed on the pub, seeing the problems John had with the Wormgate. I even went to the brewery and had interviews. Betty and I even went looking at pubs on the market. But I am getting ahead of myself.

CIVVY STREET

Azzaro who'd by now left the R.A.F. Couldn't sign on as his exit year was full. He'd joined Marconi and was working in Saudi Arabia, Khamis Mushyat installing a 40T2 Radar. He'd tried to get me to leave the RAF and join Marconi while I was at Bishops Court. Looking after me again. I did apply for personal volunteer redundancy, but it took that long to get an answer and I'd re-thought it so many times I binned the Idea. With hindsight it was the right decision for me. Funny enough when he was flying out I accompanied him to Heathrow. (in uniform) and went with him right through to the gate. Even tried the sniffer gate which was set up just before the boarding ramp.

But it's now 1982 an I am looking for a job and the recession was in full swing and interest rates were about eighteen per cent. So I asked John about a job. There's a moratorium on recruitment at the moment and if you apply they will turn you down. Then if you re-apply in better times they will see that they have turned you down before and will do so again; without reference as to why.

I went down to Cossar in Harlow and had a job interview for an Airfield Radar based on a Japanese design. I thought I'd done alright but I fancy the letter they asked me to write on my early life history sent that job down the tubes. I had several interviews and wrote many letters. Even applied for a job on an oil-rig. But no joy. I was doing a bit on the side for Chris Sims on the cottages at Tilney All Saints, so I wasn't desperate. I'd got my gratuity from the RAF. Settled some on the kids. Bought things for the home. Gave Betty some to waste. But I still needed to work.

I'd heard about Lockheed in Saudi and applied. Went down to London for the interview and the tests and passed with flying colours. Unaware that as an ex serviceman I was already accepted. One couldn't fail! We were given a briefing at a London Airport hotel on the facilities out there. i.e. Villas, pools, mess halls,transport, and the Saudi culture. We were then sent down to Bath for a course on the Saudi Radars. The 40T2 Radar was built by AEI and they were part of a deal. Your darling Harold had cancelled the TSR2 aircraft that was to be the next generation of home grown aircraft. We couldn't sell them abroad because the then Prime Minister Lord Hume had died and nobody to sign the OK price. Harold then decided to buy the American Swing wing fighter and to assist us to raise the necessary dollars we were given the Radar contract in Saudi basically by the Americans. Accommodated in a pleasant hotel in Bath and bussed to Batheaston each day for the course. There was only Marcus Anderson and I in our class and Jeff the instructor. We began with Tutorial Instruction Techniques as we were to teach the Saudi's how to do it. (Radar): before going on to the 40T2 itself. Weekends back home in my Colt, dropping Marcus at the railway station for his trip back to landampness in Welsh Wales somewhere. It was all over too quick and the personnel manager came down to see us. Expecting us to remain at the hotel before flying out on the Monday. Sod that for a game of soldiers. I'm off home. See you at the airport Marcus. All the family came to see me off, being quite a big adventure. Flying Saudi Air: (dry of course) to Riyadh. We were met by a Lockheed rep and driven to a compound and settled in. This was for a few days until posted and processed.

RIYADH

It was a bit of a wrench finding oneself without a friendly pub to go to. Lockheed had set up a bloke to show us around. Trip down to see the Gold Souks. They were quite a sight. He also nursemaided us through the intros and the when and where. Then Marcus and I were off to Dhahran. Another Saudi flight and met by Bill of H.R. More forms to fill in and escorted to a villa. Meals at 05:30 and 17:00hrs. No lunch. A man only needs two meals a day. Tell that to the Marines! Transport to work. Minibusses leave outside the mess at 0600hrs. Find some one to take you in.

Marcus and I settled in. Four man villa. Kitchen, lounge bedrooms and two shower rooms. Still feeling odd not having a drink or a place to get one. The next morning we travelled to the GEWCC workshop, about four miles away. Workshop indeed with mechanical things going on, Admin offices etc. Being Lockheed, management was ex American servicemen. John Bauman being a short arsed Texan boss and Grady Watford, about as bright as a

141

wooden cigar store Indian as his sidekick. A brit. Jeff Pritchard being the favoured one as foreman. Basically because Jeff was accompanied and Bauman was boning his missus, Jean.

We were shown to a room full of desks and benches with Tom Galbraith i/c British UHF which was the Comms kit in use and his three men who repaired the kit if returned for the same. An admin guy and the Radar section, being Martin Pitcher and Ray Milner the Marconi Engineer. We were introduced and the admin guy shouted. Aren't you going to offer them tea? Oh say Ray. Have you got any cups? We've only been in country three days and the answer is no! Well he say. No tea, going back to his book. The routine apart from turning up was there was no routine. The Radar section was expected to service the turntables of the five Kingdom radars and assist if called on for any problems the site personnel couldn't handle. Fine. Turntables are strictly a mechanical task, not Electronic and as new boys never having seen the beast the on site staff were better qualified to fix the same. But that was the way it worked apart from the weekly task of going down to store and taking the Ion Pump readings on the spare Twystron Valves used as transmitters. Mind numbing. Thought I'd learn Arabic to while away the hours. Gave it up for lack of a teacher. Martin and Milner left and Marcus and I became the new experts. Lockheed were looking for a superintendent to oversee us. We gradually got to know people and the highlight of the week was an invite to the 'officers mess' as Tom Galbraith called his villa for a drink. It was discovered that most of the villas brewed their own beer. Cannabis, though not rife was available. Likewise the locally distilled spirit know as Sid. Siddiki being the Arabic for friend. One could use the local minibusses which were loosely controlled by the assigned driver. First of course a driving licence should be obtained. That took all day. We asipirants were takedto the local hospital where ones blood group was determined and a pint had to be donated to the local transfusion service. Then the eye test. We all sat in a room together and the card. A series of E's of varying sizes and positions with the centre bar being equal to all the others. Your name was called an you stood up and responded to the pointer. Peed off the doctor when he realised that one Asian had his mate whispering the answers; but a bit too loud. He failed. Next round to the issuing authority. More forms, photos, money handed over and job done. Took all day. What a palaver.

We wore distinctive clothing, being a tailess shirt in sickly yellow and brown trousers. Safety boots. One was given $25 for a pair. Upgrade with your own money.

Lockheed was a good employer per se. The compound had cctv and the tapes were American TV shows which were just about the worst form of television one can get. Worse that even ours has become. They paid a local Brit to change the tapes and arrange the programmes. Food was reasonable. We had a pool and a library, mostly books people had brought back. I'd drop mine in there when I'd finished with them. Stan said ta very much. I found out later he was supposed to pay me for them. Not very much. He probably pocketed it, mean old sod!

We did discover a beach. About twenty klicks away Ras Tanura. We'd take a Toyota fitted with sand tyres up there. Jeff whom we called navy for obvious reasons. He was in our villa. I'd moved in with Tom. (brewing villa). Alex Keenan the rigger and yours truly and maybe one more. Alex would go Oyster hunting and Jeff and I would swim. Then Alex would return with a bunch of Oysters and I'd open them and Jeff would go through them looking for Pearls. We only found a few seed Pearls, but it gave us a day out. One Friday we'd barely started opening the things when the knife slipped and I cut my palm. Through the Artery. Blood spurting everywhere. Called everyone and with me holding my thumb over the wound rushed back and over to Aramco where for fortune there was a doctor on duty who stitched me up. Six stitches.

It was the 'officers mess' penchant to play Tennis on Friday afternoons. Doubles. Old man's Tennis. Well something went in my leg and I was on the court floor. Eased enough after a spell for me to limp back to the villa. Saw the doc next day and told the tale. He said to me the only way you play Tennis is from the viewing gallery. Ten days off work and Ibuferin and a walking stick. That was even more boring than going in to work. At least one could sneak up the airport and get a Telegraph and copy the crossword to hand out. And one could persuade the local Arab to get some beefburgers for lunch. Then came TDY as the Americans called it. Temporary duty. The Radar at Tabuk was due it's annual service. Turntables.

TABUK

It's about the 10th of December and we're flown Saudia via Riyadh but no getting off. I asked the ground controller why not? He say if I let my people off they will think they've arrived and wander off. Now came the hard part. The compound super would billet us where he had room. So we were split up. Nobody was going to lend us transport. One couldn't get a drink. Nobody wanted us. The whole thing was the pits. There were vehicles at all the sites of course and most site were in the mountains. Tabuk itself is flat as a pancake. One could put a level on the ground and it would show level. What did one drive there? Eight cylinder Landrovers. Fortunately the bloke in charge of the Radar was Al Laverty, whom I was on shift with at RAF Buchan. Thus we were reacquainted I would travel in with him and then take the Landrover back to collect my troops. Being Marcus and a rigger Brian, he had the mind of a child, and a mechanical guy. No start work until the Saudis brought in an American TPS34 as temporary cover.

Actually it was sitting there but no one to work it. So why stay? Stay you will said Bauman. You'll never know when they will turn up. I kept a diary. EMNT early morning nautical twilight. No TPS available. Some work for our Rigger Brian and we assisted on the ground. We fancy that although as Muslims Saudi's don't celebrate Christmas but taking the time off seemed a good wheeze. At last we were able to begin the servicing.

Having Al Laverty made a big difference and we got the job done eventually. Basically an oil change. Problem was. Being an English Radar, Shell Lub Oil was specified which wasn't available. Talking to the storeman he said that to import Shell oil into a Kingdom that was virtually awash with the stuff and had it's own University of Oil for want of a better expression. But nobody was prepared to offer an alternative. We got it in the end.

Tabuk town still had the remains of the railway that Lawrence of Arabia blew up. The airfield was also nicely placed for Israeli pilots to fly down the Red Sea below Radar cover and pop up and do wheelies down the runway. It was also where the Israeli's rang the Station Commander to tell him his Radar was going off for servicing. It was near there that they crossed on there way to bomb the Iranian Nuclear installation. But I digress. Divertissements were provided by Whittaker's. They were a company that supplied nurses to the local hospital and their bus would stop at the Lockheed compound to drop off any nurses that were 'courting' or simply going for a drink.

On return to GEWCC John Bauman told me that Rashid; the Pakistani advisor to the Saudi Major, was not happy with the length of time we were away. I simply gave him my diary. Glad you did that said John. Saved a lot of explanations. I had to write a report anyway. The other thing that occurred at Tabuk was that I met Major Raadi. His goal in life was to make the Radars 'Blue'. Run by the Saudi's. I asked him which was the next one on his list. He replied I have managed one. (Khamis Mushyat) but realistically don't expect to manage anymore. You can't really expect a man who was raised in a desert environment to understand mechanics: let alone electronics.

Fair comment. So back to sitting at a desk with nowt to do apart from Oyster catching at weekends. The manager John Bauman liked to visit our villa with Jeff Pritchard and his wife Jean. Other visitors were discouraged. Trouble was once Jeff had had a drink he liked to sing and the others encouraged him. Myself thought it was dreadful. They were all nice people really. Just making the best of it. The next TDY was Taif. Grady Watford issued us with Kingdom-wide passes with the injunction. If you lose them don't bother telling anyone. Just take yourself off to the local jail. Taif is about halfway down the Kingdom on the Red Sea side, Mountain about 6000' Radar perched on the escarpment. One could see the Christian Bypass round Mecca. The compound was better organised from our point of view in that the compound super had a mini bus for us, and showed us how to get up to the Radar. The grub was better too, more of it. And, there was a drinking villa that kept open house. One helped oneself and put some money in the jar afterwards. Tom was the Lockheed man and Malcolm Thomas the Marconi man. I was expected to keep a record and write a report. We were going to sandblast the structure and paint it from White to Sand Brown. Stan was the painter and a more bolshie little sod you'd be hard to find. Couple of riggers and of course Marcus.

We had to erect some zip-up staging and that was a puzzle but managed it eventually. We were there about three weeks. I was needing something and asked one of the Saudi officers who replied, don't be silly, you think we have an organisation here? One of their problems was that although I outrank you I come from a less senior tribe. We also did a modification on the Radar with some sketchy notes on how to. Marcus however did a fine job. Worked

146

straight off the bat. I enjoyed the place but was glad to return as I was going on leave...after four months get home and see the kids. Lockheed would pay for an air ticket to your home of record. Conversely Egypt Air was running a scam. Book with them which included overnight in Cairo at their expense and the fare was £100 cheaper. Lockheed would pay you this £100 saving on the home of record fare. Good eh! I never did, as I thought I wanted all my leave. The BA as we referred to British Airways was a better deal as they started serving drinks as soon as we cleared Saudi Airspace. Good Party. One trip and BA were offering a hire car. Still out of my tree I asked the young lady for a Jaguar. She apologised being fresh out of them.

RELIGION

The Saudi's being the keepers of the the Muslim Holy places and the hajjis you might say was in your face. At work when it was prayer time (five a day) one was to clean all the body orifices and to see them in the wash room hawking and spitting was enough to put one off for life.
If you were shopping at prayer time the Matawa's (religious police) would be around with their thin cane ensuring the shopkeepers closed up. A curtain across the door usually sufficed. Ramadan the fasting month saw more of them lying about sleeping during the day. And one time after the EID holiday at the end the Post Office staff simply burned the mail as being too much to handle. Cheers pal! But us Christians were there to help and were treated politely enough. When you think that we started at 0600 and RSAF Royal Saudi Airforce came in at 0700 and went home at 1300 while we stayed until 1500. Whose Air Force was it?

The next trip was only up the road to Dhahran. We took Alex Keenan a rigger. These boys will climb rigging or hang out over space fearlessly. The radar sat on a hill. More of an oversize pimple really. The road up to it was controlled by a traffic light. Press the tit and the other end knew you were coming. As they wouldn't know otherwise. Alex took one look at this and insisted on getting off and walking up. Going down from the top there was only space in front of the bonnet and didn't become road until you were at 45 degrees, and down the bottom someone had built a concrete arresting wall of such dimensions that to hit it would be fatal. Brian Baker was the site engineer and Mike Knights and Mike??? as the team. Brian knew his Radars and made the job easy. Back to sitting on chuff in GEWCC. And so it went on. We shared the brewing between the four of us and all chipped in for the sugar. All our water was filtered by ourselves and we made a passable brew. Some villas merely refilled the dustbin (Plastic) with a new mix. Some even had lumps floating in theirs.

Lockheed itself was a fair employer but I was out of sorts. I'd spent twenty-two years in an organisation where I knew my place, my job: what expectations of promotion and good camaraderie. I was now my own man along with all the other ex servicemen some of which had reverted to type some a very basic type: and to say the least; a bit lost and very unhappy! No choice but to buckle to it or do a runner.

JABAL SE' HAAN

Another job and this time to Khamis Mushayt (Thursday Market). We flew to Abha. Saudia of course with Bert Brown reassuringly as pilot. Some of the Saudi pilots were good at controlled crashes. (Landings).
SW corner near the Yemini border and were met by the Lockheed man and settled in. This was the Kingdoms 'Blue Radar' and sat on the Jabal (Jebel) at 8600ft. It was also the one that John Azzaro had helped install and commission and became the resident Marconi Engineer accompanied

by Gwen. She loathed the place. It was 100% Arab. No western influence at all.

Getting out of the car at site and the Radar was going round 350 degrees-clunk, 350 degrees-clunk. Oh! Shit! Turn it off. They hadn't noticed or got used to it and never gave it a thought. The Lockheed man was only called to site if the local boys couldn't manage the problem.

Phone calls to John Bauman to winkle out the Chief Mechanical Engineer from his eyrie at Riyadh and send a mechanical man from GEWCC. The Chief Engineer came and said he would write the report and I would do the job. No way hosay I'm not engines. He was never going to get his hands dirty. Chap came down from GEWCC and we drained the gearboxes of oil so we could get at it. Basically the turntable was driven by two electric motors mounted at 180 degrees operating through fluid clutches driving a triple reduction gearbox. Simple. One of the gears had a broken tooth and it was just a case of getting it off the shaft where it had been shrunk on and fitting a spare. Can't remember how. I sent Marcus back to Dhahran and a month later was able to join him. The Saudi crew were all nice people and we had many a discussion on polygamy women's place in their society while drinking delicious Mint Tea. Telling the joke about the Saudi's going to war with Iraq and giving the Koreans the contract. Came close to true when it did happen and half the Western world was contracted to wage it!

Another beautiful place in the mountains. Provided you ignored the Camel Spiders. Step over the sleeping guard quietly while you swapped your pass for an on site one. Speak more Arabic because they didn't do English.

RIYADH

Next was Riyadh and the Radar there. Riyadh is about

central and where it all happens from the Royalty point of view. John Bauman decided that Alex Keenan and I would drive to Riyadh thus ensuring we had transport. The rest of the crew to fly. We were given a rough sort of map on how to find the Lockheed compound, some 300 miles. Getting there wasn't too bad. They do have petrol stations and transport cafes. Problem was once we got to Riyadh we got a bit lost. Who to ask? We had no Arabic to speak of and then Manna: we not only found a Brit but he knew where the compound was. I wouldn't mind but when we got there it wasn't even identified. But they were full and they put us in an apartment block. Apartment? The corridor was 90 ft long. Huge bedrooms and bathrooms. It was a palace. The food was good too. Next day to the Radar and meet Pete Ramsay the Lockheed man and a bit later Bill Reynard who had just returned from the Pillipines and wanted to show me his holiday snaps. I wanted to know the state of play with the Radar. What spares were needed and had our kit arrived? Once Reynard had wandered off I was able to get down to brass tacks with Pete Ramsay. The job went off O.K. as we were quite clewed up on the damn thing by now and Alex and I made the run back to Dhahran.

And then they lost the contract. Boy there was some celebrating that day amongst us. The Saudi's had awarded it to D'alla Avgo. They had the airport cleaning contract. A firm from the UK was called in to recruit from the existing workforce. New Compound, paid in Saudi Riyals, same four leaves a year. I didn't fancy it. As I said my biggest problem was having spent 22 years in the R.A.F. where you were part of a family: respected, knew your place and how the system worked. Although the GEWCC workforce were exclusively ex service personnel, it was fractured and some individuals became a bit far out. Reverted to type and not very pleasant ones.

So time to pack' Lockheed would ship ones goods home and boxes and crates were brought round the villas.

Bombshell! The Radar at Taif needs servicing so off you go. Crumbs we're finished. We went. Stan the bolshie sod made a point of coming round to see me to state categorically not to expect any work out of him. Another complication was the Arab. He was supposed to be our technician and we were teaching him Radars. Joke. They have no technical knowledge. No meccano sets in the desert. He asked me, once he knew he was coming, to arrange his flights until I pointed out that as a member of RSAF (Royal Saudi Airforce) he should organise his own movements. I stressed that once we got there he would have to work. Rashid the Paki advisor would be taking an interest. That worried him My last leave I'd bought myself a new Tissot watch £100. Betty and I had a row (surprise) and I bought it to spite her. Along with an attractive plastic one £7, for work one might say.

LAST JOB TAIF

Usual scramble to board the aircraft. Arabs don't believe in queues and to wrest a vehicle for the 30k's to site. I had Alex Keenan and John Bloomfield as riggers and Tony Bond, Marcus having left, me as techs, the Bolsevik Stan and a mechanical man. I'd finely got Lockheed to send one with me. The job was now routine and for some reason I'd lent Alex my plastic watch. When we left Alex was wearing a Rolex. Somebody had taken a fancy to my plastic one and swapped his Rolex for it. He'll want it back in the morning thought Alex. But the chap had disappeared. Probably a visitor from another compound. Should have been my Rolex after all it was my plastic watch that was swapped. John Bloomfield got himself laid and was feeling a bit sheepish about it. When I got back the lads in the villa had packed my box and sent it off. They included a coffee table from the villa and a picture I'd always admired. The coffee table finished up at Clapper lane and the picture hung on the wall at utopia. The absolute final job was at Dhahran. The turntable there was making funny noises and we were sent up to shufti. Because of the shortness of time we had two shifts working 24hrs to sort it. I even had a call from a prince?? because of the proximity of the Iraq/Iran conflict. Never did get it sorted, Time to go home.

We left the compound after a long day boozing: there being nothing to do. About 5pm and flew to Riyadh where we all cleared immigration. Thence we flew to Jeddah and were transferred by mobile lounges to another Saudia flight. (dry) and home to LHR. Deplanning to find some of the Taif boys already three sheets to the wind. Fast work!

The man who never paid me for the library book, Stan. His BA flight went technical and he along with others were put up in a hotel in Dammam where the frozen steaks he had in his bag lifted from the dining hall defrosted and buggered up his baggage No wonder the food at Dhahran was the worst in the kingdom. I met Bill Dewis again whom I'd served with at West Drayton. In fact we sat together by chance flight home and did some catching up. Never saw Laverty. He was sent down to the Oman by Marconi. Mick Tracey whom went all the way back to Buchan was also there.

Nice to be home. My letter of notice (ie your sacked) was in both English and Arabic and I had to do some fast talking in the dole office to get my entitlement. One had to pay reduced N.I. even abroad to cover this eventuality. But I nearly never got it! Bloody thieves.

KINGS LYNN

So what now? Thought I wanted a pub. Pub? I'd seen

the problems that John had in the Wormgate. I must have been out of my tree. And of course to work in proximity with Betty when we were estranged enough to say the least was flying in the face of fortune. Considering that in spite of job interviews, I was never offered a position. So a pub. The way to a pub then was via the brewery direct or a broker.

Norwich Brewery offered me the Spade and Becket in March. Said it was full of Gypsies and they wanted throwing out. Didn't fancy that. Betty and I toured looking at pubs on the market. One didn't advertise them as estate agents, so one sneaked in and had a peek. We went to one in Wymondam that was being looked after by a local landlord. There was virtually no custom but it looked a good bet. So we were of to see the broker in Colchester who suggested that we look at one on Harwich docks. Driving up there from Clochester I realised I was fed up with the game and we went home. Interviews with Elgoods Brewery were productive and the Blue Boar at Eye looked the business. I didn't want to be too far away from Janine, thinking that she was a bit young to leave or expect her to come with us. No doubt really that she would have been as right as rain. Then the Live and Let Live came up and I applied for that and got it. Strangely enough the man that interviewed us for the Blue Boar intended to offer it to us. He was the same bloke that had given John the Wormgate and told John so. I wonder? What if I'd taken that?

The bank manager gave me a hard time over the extra finance I wanted and Janine gave me back her bond that I'd given her when I'd got my gratuity from the RAF. I don't think she ever got it back. Under the circumstances it's hardly surprising. The Live was a Norwich Brewery pub and the last bloke got out because they wanted to put his rent up to £1200 a week. Which was my rent. Plus it had to be on direct debit. And, a weeks course at the brewery on how to run your pub. £400. Where to stay? Sort yourself out or run backwards and forwards from your pub. How will we manage being both away. Get someone in. In the end I went and Betty did lunchtimes before my return in the evening. It was pretty exhausting and there were about nine other hopeful new publicians there doing likewise. Apart from the V.A.T, man who looked like a bearded sailor and was as queer as a nine bob note. All the ladies loved him.

 The course from my point of view was a complete waste of time. To rub it in we were taken to a promotion pub. (every time your takings exceed a median your rent will go up). Fall below and it will remain unchanged. Then we were pleased to meet Rodney Mann and buy him dinner. What Gall! The robber barons of old England were alive and well masquerading as brewers.

So we settled in to the pub. The cleaner left before we started: though I'd have been happy for her to stay. Betty was never going to do any cleaning. I'll have that microwave upstairs. But it's for heating pies etc. Bollocks to that: upstairs. In the event we barely sold any grub. The pub had a football team. Sunday League. Just my luck. But I never saw any of them. The first crowd I had in the public were playing cards and it was well after time. Eventually I got them out but they never came back. A man came in the pubic bar one night with his hand out. Said give me my darts. Darts? Where? Down there. Are you coming? No I said fed up being bullied. Right he say you've lost your dart team. Thank Goodness for that. I did go with them but not that night. The job seemed to be, providing their transport, buying their beer, buying the prizes and putting up with their banalities.

Same with the ladies team. They would form relationships and break them virtually over night. Three months into it and the landlord of the Lord Napier called me over. (you could see his pub from mine). In fact there were seven in spitting distance. Told me that the football team had been to see him and asked to play for him.

He told them to piss off. What was the matter with the Live? Well we put a bloke in there and he reported back that he didn't like the look of me and didn't feel they could come back. The Lord Napier's guvnor said he's only a man go and talk to him. They sent the captains dad. I was peeved but needed a dozen men drinking on Sundays. I was expected to go and watch them play on a Sunday morning. The absurdity of this was standing on the touchline on foggy February morning (I could have been in bed). and having to ask one of the other three spectators which team was 'mine'? I think it's them. Bloody farce. After a few weeks they wanted me to buy them a ball. Enough. Piss off and find another mug. At least the rugby team ran it's own raffles and funding. And quaffed beer!

Then there are people coming through the door whom you know right away that they are not customers. Mostly salesmen flogging cleaning products. Had a man come in one day. Royalties. Royalties? Yes. Do you play any music? I have a juke box. No that's covered by the juke box people. Any other source of music? Well I have my radio on when I'm cleaning the pub in the mornings. Can anybody hear it? By now I was beginning to catch his drift. No I say. Why should the radio be a problem? It will attract royalties should anyone hear it. Sod you mate. The BBC already pays the royalties so don't expect me to pay them again. Then a man selling beer. A new light ale bound to be a best seller. I cannot buy anything from you I am tied to the brewery. More's the pity. They sell their beer cheaper to their own houses than they sell to me. The man from the brewery. Ah good oh! He promptly produces a chart showing that this quarters sales are down on the same period last year. The last landlord had the police in here after hours as their favourite watering hole. Bit difficult to compete with that. Any way I'm not having that sales target crap stuffed down my throat. Hoppit! They gave an award to a pub in Snettisham for increased sales. The fact that the landlady of the Queen Vic had lost her husband and was struggling to manage the pub on her own and her loss of sales made the award to the pub that took her deserting drinkers. There was no more beer being delivered to Snettisham anyway. There was a time when the brewery give a landlady a widows year. i.e. if she remarried she could stay or go as she wished; or maybe the new man would take the pub on as well as her and make a go of it. Then insurance salesmen, sellers of glass washers. No Ta! It will be law soon best you buy now. Hoppit!

The cigarette machine sellers. You must have one save you bothering. No I say but they are bothering you for change for the machine. You don't have to fill them up either. I prefer to sell direct and remove the cellophane to stop them leaving it in the ashtray and risking fire. PISS OFF.

There was an old boy come in with his dog and sit quietly over a pint of mild. He wasn't down and out but out of work. No trouble couple of pints over the morning. Couple of young women came in looking for a man to do some work and I put him on to them. Casual arrangement was made. He lasted two days. Didn't really want to work. Down and outs in the public Thursdays, when they got their dole cheques. I had to throw them out in the end. They prevent a more respectable type of customer using the place.

Once the various dart and crib leagues had finished the Public bar was a desert. I said to Betty you go down and open up and I'll come down later. The noise drove me down. There was a host of Irish Tinkers trashing the place. I threw them out. Next time I came down and the place was full of skinheads the eldest being about fifteen. Why did you serve them? Well he was only one and then the rest followed. Of course one to test the water and the others follow. Right lads enjoy your drink because there aint no more. Don't leave glasses in the sink with the water one cannot see them and a quick wash and I've broken a glass and probably cut myself. Talk to the wall. Betty never really understood any of it.

I'd had a bellyful. Worse days work I ever did. We were quietly going broke. I was obviously not cut out to be a publican. Luckily we still had Reffley. Many people would sell up to pay for the pub and were stuck with them. Mick and Pat were living in the Reffley waiting to go to Spain. He took me to see his son John pass out at square bashing. T'was a Summers day. We were all lined up at the viewing stand and the Station Commander made a short address, where he said that when he joined the RAF twenty-two years ago etc and was now a Group Captain. I thought. Where did I go wrong? I only made chief technician.

He then said, however there is a recruit passing out today that has more clout in this mans airforce than I because he has arranged a Harrier Fly-past. Terry Parker the pilot had pulled strings to do this for John. The C.O. did warn Mum's with babies and children that it would happen very sudden and with a lot of noise. So watch out!

After the parade the Sun was shining and there was a light aircraft stooging about and we all retired to the NAAFI to talk to servicemen about our son's future. I was only a guest so no to talking. I was wrapped in nostalgia and even more determined to quit the pub. Once we'd got back I rang a broker and asked him to find a new hopeful. He explained that the queue of people wanting pubs had become very short. Whereas before, the brewery could pick and choose, now, they were grateful to take anybody. I could give it back to the brewery but would only get bare bones for it. They were already taking half the takings from the bandit and then they'd come up with a wheeze that all us publicans would chip in (mandatory) so they could paint their pubs and keep them looking nice. Yes we'll do yours in the fulness of time! I'd had a bellyful and was trapped. What with Betty's intransigence and having to open that dammed door because it was my livelihood. And have the same conversation with the same bloke I'd had yesterday.

Then one morning Azzaro walks in the door with Gwen as large as life. I thought you were in Jordan? I am, but I get home from time to time, especially as I am the project manager. Gwen, as he always did. Go behind the bar. You come with me and I'll tell you what I want. So we had a mini pub crawl: the upshot being that he wanted me in Jordan with him as someone who could do the job. Here's an application form. Fill it in, it's all arranged and settled. Lifeline. Bloody miracle! Bless you Azzaro you've done it again. The form was filled in and posted off and I went down to see Harry Gill the under manager for Field Services at Marconi Chelmsford. Basically we sat and had a chat and he got personnel to take me over and do the business there and they'd give me shout when my security clearance came through. I'd signed the offical secrets act.

Nothing happened! Weeks went by and eventually I received a call to report to Writtle Road on Aug 12 1985 to become a field engineer for Marconi. Heady stuff indeed. I went over and saw a solicitor and arranged for Betty to have power of attorney so she could sell the pub, or piss off and leave it. Same same the house and while your doing all that arrange me a divorce. No problem. I'd opened an account with the Midland bank as it was then in Kings Lynn and never told a soul apart from payroll. Reporting to Chelmsford I was informed that due to the length of time it took to get my security clearance I wasn't going to Jordan. They sent me to Rivenhall test site. Basically an ex wartime airfield where they had three brand spanking new Radars being produced for NATO. The farmer had the soft bits and we the hard. There was a canteen on site and the village of Silver End was a mile away where we were accommodated in the Silver End Hotel. Surprise. (now an old peoples home) At the time it was run by an Australian couple. A bit run down but adequate. The engineers on site made me welcome and my spirit climbed out of the pit it had been in. The security clearance problem was because I'd gone to Saudi Arabia with Lockheed. I'd done twenty-two years in the R.A.F. And signed the official secrets act. But it was a blessing in disguise.

John Norman was the man in charge of the Radar at White gates. Merely a designation on the airfield. There was a Dave Watts from South Africa and Dave Allton and Paul ???. It was a joy. I'd run across to see Alec and Sally weekends. The M25 wasn't finished so it was a bit tricky at times. After a couple of weeks I was feeling quite chagrined at leaving Betty. Especially with the pub and all and I decided to run back up and see her. Sally was incensed: but not yet up, and before she could rise and stop me, I was gone. Told them in the pub I'd been down at St Mawgan incomunicado. But in truth there was nothing left of the marriage. We were never going to have more than a difficult relationship. A continuance one might say. So I left her and she was devastated once the truth of it hit her. No doubt the pub was the catalyst and Azzaro the prime mover I didn't enjoy it but it had to be done. We'd reached that point in time. I'd always said I'd go once the kids had left home.

So here I am back doing what I always enjoyed. Working on Radars. Or as Dave Watts said one day. Toys for grown up boys. Then Harry Gill phoned me and said I am going to change your lifestyle. Send me the first four pages of your passport. I am sending you to the Oman. Shit, John said don't let him, but I had no choice. I'd little left of the £200 I'd taken from the till in the pub but the DMA about £20 per diem helped and the last weekend at Sally's I gave her my first fortnights wages for Rosa. Rosa being her sister who life had dealt a very poor hand. She was short. Had no looks. Picked men that beat her up Was being evicted. Alec had no time for her. So here's a cheque Sal. I'm off now. That's for all your help and support in the past!

MUSCAT OMAN

Sits directly under the Tropic of Cancer and is fiercely hot in Summer. Muscat is well served with roads, landscaped gardens, trees, fountains amongst stark barren mountains. I was met of course and taken to the managers office to meet Ken Allender boss man and John McDonald the chief engineer. He said to me. Enjoy the capital area because in about three months I'll transfer you to Thumrait. I rotate my engineers from the more basic sites. The admin guy Dave ?? processed me, immigration, fingerprints, driving licence (civil). Military one required a test. photographed for my passes and handed a wodge of local currency. I was given a room in a block with sixteen of them. Four either side and the ablutions in the middle. Same upstairs. My shift partner was Potty Bobby and Duff gen Den and the Radar was up a low mountain. Each shift had a White Toyota which could also be used for recreational purposes. Petrol from the military was free and pennies if you ran short in town.

So there I am. Forty-two years of age and of no fixed abode. Got a job yes and accommodated out there pro tem. The gods had been kind. By denying me Jordan and sending me to Oman where there was an eighty-seven and a half uplift on one's salary. Tax free and nine local Riyals per diem: I was able to start again as it were

So we settled in and life was good. Danny Joseph was the site engineer and Don (filthy) Firth from Rivenhall was there. Friendly crowd and we got on well being about twenty or so. Split of course. Some in MAM and some at Bowshar with their wives. We had a mess and a bar we shared with BAe and the Comms people. Beer was cheap and you were licensed to drink ten percent of your salary. Though never checked or enforced. Food was superb, the

160

catering budget seemed endless. People from the sub continent made up the bulk of the cheap labour, waiters, cleaners, bar staff etc. Baluchistani's the uniformed security. Worked and passed my military driving test, very much a simple English style affair. The civil one was issued against my International One. Christmas and Danny Joseph invited us to Bowshar where the married types lived. He was married to a Danish girl whom he'd met in Bornholm. I'd met him briefly in Dhahran went he was sent out as Marconi Engineer on the Dhahran Radar but he was declared PNG by the Saudi's much to his relief. Gave us a good night in their club and Christmas Day found me playing Golf of a sort with George Wallace. Good Eh!

Come January I was having a spot of leave. Colin was getting married to Elaine whom he met in the Live and I wanted to go obviously. How will it be when I get back to Lynn? Can't go to the Reffley. Ah! Fly KLM to Amsterdam, and Amsterdam to Norwich. If Betty plays up rough I'll fly back to AMS and finish my leave there. I was overnight in the Port Van Cleef compliments of KLM.

Phoned Betty to ascertain the wedding arrangements and me/her relationship. Down for dinner and a pre prandial. Met Mr Heineken and got his card to pin up in the Marconi bar in Oman. Silly really. Quick visit to the Red Light district to reacquaint myself with the opposite sex. Flew to Norwich, got a taxi to Lynn and the Dukes Head. Booked in and contacted Betty. She was all sweetness and light and we even went round to the Live for a drink and to discuss Colin's coming nuptials. Kings Lynn R.O. then an evening bash at the North Star p.h. in North Lynn. Not a particularly salubrious place but I wasn't organising it. Then round to see Paul Selwood at work, where she confirmed that I would be staying with them at Utopia: as in her words. I certainly couldn't afford to stay in the Dukes. Maggie had made up a truckle bed for me in the lounge. Talk about the architect of ones downfall. From moving on to the Reffley in '74, where we had neighbourhood parties to get to know each other I was well taken with Maggie. It went on to friendship. I liked Paul well enough. We'd done the Steam Engine show at Stradsett. Gone fishing. Were in and out of each others houses and as much as I was attracted to Maggie: we never mentioned it. Even to each other. Though at times I could barely keep my hands off her!

Having a drink in the Dukes or somewhere come a bleak January. The day of the wedding with the ex in laws. Dink and Jim Logie, Andrew, Janine and Kevin. Edna came in and I thought: here we go. Why did you leave Betty after all these years? Never mentioned it. We simply chatted about this and that as one does. The ceremony went down well enough as it always did in the Lynn R.O. And we wasted time until time for the North Star. This'll be fun I thought. North Lynn (Gyro City). In the event it turned out well. Good disco, dancing. Maggie said I was ignoring her. I was trying to keep the proprieties. Poor Colin had a severe tummy bug. Spoilt the night for him. Must have been an Omen for the marriage. I hired a car the next day just for getting about. Lunched with Kevin and Janine and went off to see Chris Sims at the Porterhouse ph. Lynn.

The next day. 22nd Jan '86 moved out of the Dukes and over to Maggie's. A fateful Day! What to do on a cold January afternoon? Well the waters broke and we went to bed. Come the evening and Paul found an excuse to go out so we did it again. Yes Snake in the Grass. Take a man's salt and abuse his hospitality. The marriage had been in trouble for some time. Well that's my excuse and I took every advantage. I loved her desperately and had to win her hand. Others were sniffing around.

Then after a delightful interlude of being in Maggie's company and looking at houses for her and Paul. Places totally unsuitable considering the needs of his young children. Although it was Paul's affair my sympathies were with Maggie. I returned to Alec and Sally's at Ruislip. Having no cause to remain at Maggie's. We went over the Orchard and back to 11 Filey way and had a nice boosy afternoon chatting as one does. Up a dart club in the evening. Sally saying we need to find you a new partner. Fat chance I say dragging me round dart clubs.

Monday and Alec was back to work. Gave me a job stripping wallpaper, He was convinced me and Sally were sweet on each other. Sally slapped my face more than any other woman. She was good company but I never imagined her in any other role. Rang Maggie. Telly in Wellse's house was all sport. They never watched anything else.

Off to see the family. Jackie and David first at Southbourne. Lunch at The Good Intent. Wed 29th go Pompey with Jackie. Get some perfume. Do the Mary Rose. Lunch at the Still and West. Then round to see Joyce. She looked well. Janine had rung she needed £500 for a deposit. Will fix Friday. Then back to Lynn for an assignation with a certain lady. Where Paul was I don't know, but we went up the pub and back for a bit of misbehaving. Last day of January and I went up the LIVE to renew old acquaintances Betty was there and I ran her home after, where we had one of our blazing rows. Good it say in my dairy. Up the Dukes for dinner. Maggie and Paul. Betty, Janine Kevin. back to Maggie's for the last night of leave. Back to Sally and Alec next day and the night flight to Oman.

THUMRAIT

It was February and John MacDonald decided it was time for me to move to Thumrait. This was to become my second home though I never imagined it at the time. The flight down was on a SOAF BAC 1-11 and landing at Thumrait we taxied off the runway on to a sand scrape and we de planned Baggage being place on a concrete plinth between the fence separating airside from ground side. I was met by Laurie the admin fella and taken round to my accommodation which was a small room in a family bait. (villa Arabic for house). Which was not only occupied by Frank Illingworth but was the Marconi bar! There was a pub in the mess hall but this was a shebeen for after hours work. Fell on my feet you might say. They put me on shift with the brat, Dave Mobray who had been up at MAM also. As I said, you could use the vehicles for recreation. He would, while up North go to Abu Dhabi for his four days off. And Danny Joseph on day five would be saying. He's not only late for work he's not even in country! His watch mate of course was denied the use of the vehicle. Pleasant enough young man but totally unaware of social pressures or responsibilities. He and I on shift. Afternoons. Start at 1pm. Dave suggests a Salalah run in the morning and a swim in the sea. We get back about 12:45 and I'm having kittens. We need to shower, change, lunch and get to work' Left it a bit tight David. Oh, no problem, we'll only be a few minutes late.

I stopped going to Salalah with him. He went North as we called Muscat and I got Pete Winchester. Huge bear of a man, nicknamed Blutto from the popeye cartoons: but not to his face. Full beard, eighteen stone with a capacity for booze that Dean Martin would have been proud of. They also moved me to a new 'bait'. Self contained en suite room with walled garden and a door at the end to close. The doors had been put on by previous occupants so not all had them. Visiting was not encouraged. Life was good. Alan Macaneeny was the systems engineer and Dave Elliot site engineer. There also Alan Laverty who was my shifty at RAF Buchan. Roo, the Australian and Keith Child and Tony Child and Len Sparks. No relation. The Omani air force ran the site, comprised of a office building and a S600 Marconi Radar and a C band height finder. They had some controllers but mostly they were Brits ex forces and in the Omani Air force. The pilots on the Hunter squadron were also ex RAF enjoying an extended flying career. There were three vehicles for the shift workers. A white Toyota that was on mornings, a brown Toyota that was on afternoons and a Toyota truck that was on nights. Daft, but we moved the vehicles to suit the shifts. One did three afternoons followed by three mornings and three nights, followed by four days off.

GOLF

There was an eighteen hole golf course, self built with browns instead of greens. Mix oil and fine sand and you have a putting surface. One has a heavy rake and a carpet to scrape away the footprints. So I tried to learn how to hit a ball. Winch tried showing me and Tony Child also. They gave up on me and it was about a year before I could hit a true ball. It was a thriving club with sixty or so members. Decent bar and a change from the T3 one. Mel Ross brought me back an air weight bag and a set of clubs to get me going. Only snag was, one removed a club and the bag collapsed around the others and they all fell to the ground. No, no sports shops in Arabia. Squash or tennis courts were available. I tried Squash. Even with a nine start Winch beat me with ease. So I concentrated on the golf and fishing. It involved a trip to Salalah and along to the harbour. Find the boat. Fit the engine and sail out to sea. That probably took two hours. Couple out fishing and then back and undo it all. Next into the Penguin for a milkshake or into the Dhow at what was RAF Salalah for a cold beer. Lovely. Back to Thumrait usually fish less. Did get a couple of Dogfish one trip. Difficulty was in skinning them. Winch also smoked a pipe with tobacco he'd adulterated with Whisky. Most evil mixture when sharing a cab with him on the way to work. Personalised London fogs.

Then came Neil Linge from Marconi instruments. About twenty. Volunteer. Nobody volunteered for Oman too long away from home. Winch disliked him from the off and would bait him at every opportunity. Especially as he had no knowledge of radar. He was instruments, so he was a drone on shift. Anyway there were a lot of men out there married to Thai wives. Beautiful creatures who seemed to exist to please man. Neil all the way from the UK was having some, or one. He managed to wangle some leave half way through his first four months and went off to Thailand. Fixed himself up with one: came back and promptly resigned. Job Done! The manager Ken Allender was hopping mad.

Marconi graded its engineers from grade eight to thirteen. The only distinction between them apart from pay was the senior tended to get   senior/ site engineer etc. Airworks provided the ground staff for the airfield including servicing the Aircraft and armourers. They also did the admin, ran the accommodation and the cleaning staff. In fact the whole schmeer. The two bars operating in the mess were T3, named after LHR and senior stiffs. People in T3 had their names on the bar and stools to match. The place was often an inch deep in beer and I hated it. The senior stiffs was a much more civilised affair, but Airworks insisted that only nominated Marconi engineers could use it. So unless Winch was going in and taking me, I was buggered. Winch was happy in either bar I eventually convinced the stiffs that I was a member in spite of no letter.

Again food was good and I would put my local currency on top of my wardrobe and turn it into Gold before my leave. Rooms were cleaned by Blue force daily. A squad of Bangladeshi cleaners. Airworks worked from six-thirty until one thirty when the bars and dining halls opened, closing at three. Before the Air Commodore who advised this restriction, they were open from cease work until nine pm. So those of that persuasion could drink their fill, eat and go to bed and be bright eyed and bushy tailed come the morn. He (Air Com) introduced these twice open policy. Mind you one could buy anything to take out or get six beers in a bag of ice and stay there until opening time. Heaven!

So time to rebuild my life and my fortune. I'd seen too many people make lawyers wealthy fighting over the family split. I'd left Betty in the pub she didn't want and as far as I was concerned she could have the house too. I simply wanted out. As we all know she sold up and went to live with her Mother at 11 Iping and eventually giving Andrew Leaver the money to buy the place. No paper agreement. I am sorry for abandoning her, but I was truly at the end of my tether and with her intransigence over the years. on reflection I gave her a good life. I took her out of Iping Avenue and around the country with various postings. New schools, new neighbours. She was a great gossip. Malta for the foreign field and life long friends. A car? And of course the house at Reffley

A chance to settle down; become a local. And you might say I set her up in business. Feel a bit bad about that, but at least she was warm and dry. Shame the latest bloke she had her eye on upped and died. That was in the pub. My sergeant Phil Fuller would drive fifty miles to see her. Makes you wonder what she was really like in bed. But of course he was screwing me. We even went over to see him and his wife at Martham ex Saudi. After a couple in the local found me and his wife playing strip poker for fun. While he and Betty stayed in the kitchen. I remember getting up in the night and looking for Bet, as she was certainly not in my bed. Never did find out. Come the morn and me up with the Lark. No one. It was a Sunday. I went out and found a paper shop. Nobody rose before half ten. We never went again, though he popped in the pub once. I found out eventually and wrote and told his wife. She divorced the bastard!

All in all a fair swap. Three lovely kids. Now divorced

and going our own separate ways. I of course am in the Oman and writing to Maggie and making plans. She had done the decent thing and re-mortgaged Utopia so Paul could have his share of the equity; such as it was, and thus start again. (him). And us? Obviously Maggie stayed at Utopia with the children. Utopia was very basic but it was warm and dry. Jackie and David were in Southbourne expecting Oliver. Janine was still with Kevin, and Colin and Elaine were in Germany I fancy.

I sent Maggie my bank card so she could draw some money from the hole in the wall, followed by the PIN under separate cover. She wrote and said she never got the PIN. Panic! In those days the only way to make a phone call was via the military at Thumrait being patched North and again patched through to a civilian exchange. If you weren't pally with a Brit controller Nada! It worked and chatting to Maggie, it had arrived. Relief! She'd tried it too! It worked.

Then the contract was up for renewal and Ken Allender was looking for volunteers to leave the country. Leave? Put me down Ken. In fact I was on leave at home when Harry Gill rang me and said. Don't go back yet, wait for a phone call from me. We're putting the contract together and I want you to take it back with you. I got two extra days at home., Bloody magic until Allender took them off me saying I was late back off leave. Collect new ticket at ticket desk. When I fell off the aeroplane next morning, one of the Jundies. (Indian Office Wallah) handed me a torn off piece of newspaper with scribbled on it. Anything for me give to Arshad So much for the importance of the contract. The Indians were used to ferry us to and from the airport among their other duties. Well I was going home to Maggie. Magic. Then Allender rang. Mike Ball at Masirah wants out and I'm sending him. We had some heated words but I lost the day.

As much as I wanted to get back to Maggie I thought it

was time I made a visit to Uncle Con in South Africa. He was my mother's brother and we'd got on well. He was travel manager for S.A. airways at Waterfall in Natal. I'd been in touch and he was delighted at the thought. Unfortunately travel arrangements were difficult. I wanted to use my leave ticket but in the end it was fly UK and purchase another for South Africa which I wasn't prepared to do. (Fate)? So back to UK. I could always drive my kids mad by visiting them. Say in dairy. Letter Jackie. Letter Maggie. Lovely jubbly. Stop boozing with Winchester and start playing golf again. Booked car hire LHR. Pay rise 4'6%. 18 May '86, go North. Mutrah Gold Souk. See Allender. You go in June. Super. Drink Don Firth and Danny Joseph before return Thumrait.

Seem to be having problems with my golf. Can't. With my drinking. Too much. 25th June and I am in the Dukes Head. Wrote to Con explaining the change of plan but he never got it. I was going but other matters were more pressing. Checked the solicitor re divorce. Enjoyed a few days with Maggie discussing a possible future together. Then flight to Germany to see Colin and Elaine. Did the tourist bit together the next day. Copper Kettle in the evening. You go back and get the dinner ready Elaine and we'll be up directly. Sod that she say. I'm watching the World Cup! I've given you a good day, lunch. etc. So what she say. I suggested she pack a bag and I'd take her back to the UK with me. Obdurate cow! Nice to see my son looking well and enjoying Germany. Back to Ruislip for Fri 4th. Take my insurance man John Hannam to lunch at Hatch End. Next Leigh Park, Joyce out. Tea at Jackie s. Thence to Hayling for a few beers with Arthur. Haven't you got a better local than this? Yes, but this is where I bring you and Mike. We finished up rowing. Cantankerous old sod. Back to Lynn to see Maggie, staying with Mick and Pat at North Wootton. Pat suspected that I was seeing Maggie. Even though I wasn't saying. A good leave. Saw everyone and sorted things out. July, solicitor informs papers served, should be Nisi by October Letter Maggie saying she has chucked Paul out. So we're clear. Aug more good news. Jackie pregnant. Hooray!

October now and on leave. Hire car and straight to Maggie's. Taking her to Amsterdam for a few days. Had to organise her passport. Off to Peterborough to the passport office and sort that out. You could in those days. Next flight to Amsterdam. Maggie's friend Alison having the kids. Maggie's first trip abroad. Port Van Cleef in Damm Square. They're in the hospitality business not the morality business. Few days doing the tourist bit. We both enjoyed a chance to be together without interruptions. Thought I'd blown it one night on waking to see her gazing out on the wet streets of Amsterdam. Back, BA to LHR; bright sunny day and our town laid out in all it's splendour. I flew back to Oman on a BA Jumbo that was at capacity. Dreadful journey. One beer, one dinner and no sleep.

I was back at Thumrait and on shift with Al Laverty and Sparky, the town drunks. Going on nights 10pm one had to trawl round the various bars looking for them. Get them on the wagon and up to site: a wheeled chair out the office to get them inside. I never took a drink going on nights. Booze and Poorly Radars don't mix. Admin rang from the North. I'd won a camera in the Falcon mess draw. Will send by courier. Rocket brought me a Rolex from Thailand £28 I expect he made a profit but who cares. Mel Ross had his wife out for Christmas and she was walking about with her arse hanging out of her shorts. Teasing everyone. Other wives were out but all more respectable. The proprieties were observed. That was Mel's 'Spanish' wife. They divorced soon after.

THE WEDDING

Two blokes I'd been on shift with were Eric Beech and Brian Dawson both came to the wedding along with their wives, Irene and Sheila. Took a B&B locally and we all had a great night up the Coach and Horses at Tilney. Maggie had set the day. 9th May '87 Kings Lynn R.O. My guests, obviously Jackie and David. Oliver came too but he didn't know it. Janine and Kevin as it was then. John and Gwen, Alec and Sally, Mick and Pat. Arthur, bloody late. He declines Mick's offer of a bed for the night and I'll be there in the morning. No Arthur would drive up on the day. No Sandy. She had nothing to wear. Crikey who cares? He visited every pub in Lynn looking for us. Pigheaded sod! Chris Sims came for the bun fight but declined afters at Utopia. The Sun shone. It was a perfect May day. Nice do in the Wheatsheaf at Walpole and back to Utopia for an afternoons gentle boozing amongst ones friends and relations. Janine thought I be leaving my family behind for my 'new one'. I also discovered that Sally had a big soft spot for me. Maggie had her children but her mate, Alison? Took them away later as we were off to a secret location for the nuptials. Her Dad, Reg? Silvia? What a day. Went off by taxi, much, much later. The Knights Hill hotel. Had one drink at the bar. Up to the room and Look. A bed. Promptly fell into it and was asleep in seconds. So much for deflowering the bride.

We returned next morning to find that Alec and Sally who'd stayed the night had washed up and cleared all away. No honeymoon. We'd had that the week before. So back to the Oman. They were calling for volunteers to leave again as the customer wanted further reductions in manpower. I won the day this time. Flight home and Chelmsford here we come. I was sent to Clee hill with Jimmy Wright. Kevin Towers had to go to Germany as Pete Crosbie was on leave. We were upgrading a Plessey search/weather radar for the Civil Aviation authority. Enjoyable few weeks. Maggie came and we did B&B.

There was a nice pub at the bottom of the hill that had just been taken over by a London Bobby. They did good food. There was also a petrol station selling Oak petrol. Maggie and I did the Iron Bridge at Telford, and I went and looked at RAF Boot camp in Bridgnorth. This is the gate the walls are men. And that was all that was left. Ironic. Anyway we got that job done and it was back to Chelmsford where Harry sent me on home office. Go home and wait for the phone to ring,. It rang.

TURKEY

Your going to Turkey with John Matthams mechanical man and Brian Sermons, Engineer, known as sermon on the mount. Your be doing the Southern NATO chain of Radars that are in need of some improving, As in maintain while train. Doing it John Matthams way. We flew Pan-Am to Geneva and Swiss Air to Ankara. Ankara's airfield is Esenboga. The place of the Wind. Checked into the Hotel Dedeman, a well run down past it's splendour type of place. Only one night. The hire car arrived in the morning, The traffic looked frightening. (it was). Yes Parker was elected to drive with John doing the navigating and we set of for Sivas which was about half the 100km journey. Turkish roads once out of the city were poor potholed affairs for the most part. At times one would find traffic coming towards one. They were merely avoiding potholes on their side of the road. Plenty of cafe's along the route and we changed drivers at every one, reaching Sivas about eight at night. Found a hotel. Very basic and had a meal and then sat in the foyer and had a beer or two. There was no bar, but in Turkey there is always a boy to run errands. Next day we completed the run to Erzerum in short order and booked into a better hotel. There was about four feet of snow everywhere. I sent the boys back at Thumrait a piccy and a cry of woe.

The object of the exercise was to find the Radar. There were or weren't any records at Chelmsford re installed Radars. We knew it would be up a mountain. A partial run at one mountain and John and Brian decided time to fit snow chains. A must in all Turkish hire cars. Struggling to fit them while sliding about on the white stuff. Suddenly I pointed out to John and Brian that fitting snow chains on the back wheels of a Renault 12 was superfluous as it was front wheel drive. John Matthams said sod this and we returned to the hotel. The Radar there sits at 10,000ft so we were on a hiding to nothing anyway. After much phoning to Marconi and NATO in Brussels we were told to go back to Ankara and 'do' Alhatibel. Thus we did the whole trip in reverse. At least Ankara was without snow. They sent a Turkish airman to the Dedeman to show us where. We needed him. You don't have time to observe road signs in a Turkish town and drive. Having met those in charge we began. John was doing the mechanics and Brian and I the electronics. Though as the engineer he was also guiding me through the process. For lunch we didn't. In the evenings we'd wander out and find somewhere to eat. Restaurant or hotel. Some were nice and some not. We soon established a few favourites. One annoying Turkish habit is to reset the table the moment you are finished, even if your still on the coffee. One night and John announces it's his fiftieth birthday and he would treat us to a Chinese. Ad in local paper. We are asking at the desk and ordering a taxi and this woman standing at the counter said. There are no Chinese restaurants in Turkey. They are all Turkish. Well it was a bloody disaster. Wrong food at the wrong time. One for you, none for you yet. Finished up with John yelling. Take it away and bring it back H.O.T. hot! There was a small hotel I preferred and we divided our time between that and the Four Roses restaurant. Finally, job done. Reports handed over and we gratefully flew back to U.K. One days travel at home and back to Chelmsford.

A SPELL IN THE U.K.

Or so I thought. It's 1988 and with the resolution for Maggie to stop smoking we're off to see Jackie and David at Southbourne. David at football. Where else? Popped up Chestnuts in the evening. Over to see Joyce and Ron next morning for a chat and back to Lynn on Sunday. Azzaro rang. When are you back at work? I'll see you in the Miami Motel. Betty rang. Have you signed yet? I want to apply for a mortgage. Power of attorney I suppose, but she had that. I rang Bryn Morgan my 'boss' at Marconi. Probably Mardin in Kurdistan about Feb 1st. Meanwhile RAF Boulmer Monday the 11th. I rang Michael and arranged to stay with Vincent and Jackie who were in married quarters there, It's at Alnwick. Saturday took Adam and Jan Jan shopping in Wisbech; give Maggie a bit of a lie in. Sunday and Grahame the plumber came to look at the bathroom and give a price. New plastic bath etc. all very modern. I left after lunch for RAF Boulmer. About five hours. Check in and me and Vince down the Burnside for a pint.

Down the hole at Boulmer and see Nix Harrison, site engineer whom I was joining albeit temporally and start work. Bryn Morgan rang. Return 28th for one month Mardin. Popped over the Schooner in Alnmouth to see Ray Milner who said. Mardin? It's the pits. Don't go. Milner was the RME at GEWCC, Saudi Arabia. One of the lads there said that not only did Milner have the free run of the Schooners kitchen. That lass there has a rip-cord on her knickers for Milner. I moved out of Vince and Jackie's rather than wear out my welcome and moved to digs at Alnmouth. Had a night in the Sgts Mess and met some old faces. Nice evening. Left for the Mardin trip about the

22nd Jan.

TURKEY

NATO had a chain of Radar stations from the Arctic Circle   right round to Syria. All facing Russia. They NAMSA felt that the more southerly ones were not performing as well as they should and were sending a team of experts in each discipline to MWT. Maintain while train. I copped as the transmitter expert on old Marconi radars.
Thus 1st Feb found me Pan-Am to Munich and Lufthansa to Ankara. I checked in to the Metropole Hotel. We'd dined there on the last visit and I liked the place. Comfortable. Later having a beer in the bar the local harlot tried to pick me up and I was quite offended. The barman was putting her drinks on my tab. In time Belma and I would meet in the bar. Or it seemed that way whenever I was passing through she was there. She invited me back to her place once. I pointed out that I had just left Maggie or was seeing her the next day and I wasn't that interested anyway. I'd buy her a drink. Marconi pay. After that she almost became and old friend, at least a friendly face when passing through. I got a phone call from someone telling me not to travel to Mardin in the dark hours.???

Next day and it's Turkish airlines to Dyabikir and a night in the Buyuk Hotel before taxiing 90ks to Mardin the next day. The road runs along part of the Euphrates River of biblical fame. Met John Matthams there and Ken Yates doing their thing and went back with them to their hotel in Nusaybin. A nightmare ride along a road that was all tankers or lorries with rubber oil tanks in the back. No drivers hours. Earn the money. Many accidents. Good session catching up and the next day Mardin. Three radars sitting on a hill. I was moved in to the Gazino. Basically the Officers/SNCO's accommodation. It was cold. The Turks didn't seem to be able to afford to heat the place. No beer. The C.O. was strict Muslim. Water pressure nil. Hot water? Don't be silly. The duty officer would be informed that hot water is coming and there'd be me and about six Turks in the shower doing our selves and our dhobi before the hot water ran out. About forty gallons in my estimate.

The radar had not worked for three months and they were looking to me to wave a magic wand and fix it. Some chance. They never seemed to have any spares. Three radars sitting on a hill that was that steep that one was pulled up in a cage by a wire rope and a winch. In any other country it would have been a Funicular Railway. I was cold, miserable,depressed and never understood a word being spoken. Mum I want to come home. I can't remember if we ever got the damn radar working at least not properly. The Turks have a way of distorting the laws of Physics. New twist. No hot water. No water. I was sleeping fully clothed. I did manage to ring Maggie using Jetons on a local phone. To go out to cash a travellers cheque I had an armed escort. I had to pay the Gazino in Dollars. The food was cooked in a hut shed like you find in a lay-by nowadays. Placed on the counter on metal plates where it instantly cooled to ambient (cold) and was carried across to the mess by the airman doing the cooking, Talk about make life difficult. Finally we were off. Back to Ankara and civilisation and the venison of hot water. Rang Bryn Morgan to bring him up to date. Same same Maggie. Off to Pazar next on the Black Sea coast next to Georgia, Russia.

PAZAR

I flew to Trabson and hired a car for the run along the coast. I got to Pazar. A long cold wet muddy place and booked in to a hotel there. Then along to the town and find the HQ TAF. Made my number. Where's the Radar? Up the hill. Where else? My Interpreter who was now assigned to me Sabahatin Ajar and it was; go up the hill and have a look. They had it in kit form. Doing I don't know what. But introductions all round and we started work. The Turks are nice people but if you can't understand a word of the language, and your cold. It becomes bloody difficult to communicate. No telly in hotel, only Turkish, same radio. Well I was in Turkey I know. But God, I hated it. Captain Dundar from Mardin arrived doing an inspection. Said I should move into the Gazino. After my experiences at Mardin mate forget it! After some more pressure I moved. Crumbs the place was warm. There was hot water. A pair of slippers by the shower,a robe. After dinner I'd sit in splendid isolation in front of a telly watching the pictures. Bell to hand to summon a waiter for a beer. Then day three I ventured down where we ate. They were drinking beer, playing cards. Bridge, and Backgammon. Boy can the Turks play Backgammon. The dice barely get a chance to rest before being taken up for the next move. I was in. This is more like it. We didn't work weekends and Sabbhatin asked me what would I do. Go to Russia I say, it's only up the road. We went and got as far as seeing the place. The only border control appeared to be a boy goatherd. It felt strange to look at a country that had been the 'enemy' most of my life.

I threw a party there when we'd finished the job. Well I never finished. The C.O. threw me off the site for wearing Jeans. Good party though. Marconi paid though they weren't happy about it. (throwing Largesse about). Turkish airman. I want to dance with you. No! Is not custom. He was quite upset and gave me the fingers. It only cost £50 for 28 people including food and drink

I rang Harry and said I can't finish the job I've been slung off site. Come home he say. But I've got Pershembe in five days time. No matter Harry say. You deserve a weekend, we'll send return tickets to Utopia. That was decent of him. Nice four days at home with Maggie. On return they had sent Brian Sermons (Sermon on the mount) to assist. The Turks had said they didn't think I was knowledgeable enough. Crumbs. One Radar that hadn't worked for three months; the next one in kit form. What did they want? So we hired a car and went to Pershembe, on the Black sea coast. Finding a half decent hotel the Turista. Tony Child was there doing display systems and an American. Glen Henry doing the 'other' height finder. He was an American who had married a Dutch girl while serving with the American Forces in Germany. So, a bit of getting to know one another in the bar later. Brian was willing and helpful engineer in the full sense of the word. With Marconi. If you needed assistance or technical help it was freely given, No stigma attached.

Brian took charge and I actually saw or heard him give a sermon on the mount to a Turkish Technical officer. The radar was up a mountain of course. Come the weekend and we thought our Turkish was good enough; we decided to drive to Samsun and organise another car. Me and Sabbhatin to go on to Bartin and Brian and the Hertz man to Trabson and give the car back. Simple enough. Should have taken Sabbahtin. Come Wednesday No car. Get Sabbhatin on the blower to Hertz.

We took the bus to Samsum and collected a small Fiat 131 for the trip to Bartin and then Ankara. My dairy reports;- no wipers, no brakes, no washers, no lights. Nightmare. Being a late start we decided that Kastomonu was the overnight stop. We were over the mountains and there were no chains in the car. How I made it, Heaven above knows. At Kastamonu we asked the police for the best hotel and having found it told Sabba to organise accommodation. One room? No one each. Marconi pay. And back here in two mins I'm starving. Later in the bar. Sabba had wandered off and a Turk turned to me and made a remark about the football on the telly. Minor sensation got a Brit in the bar and well off the tourist trail. I was well received and the beers were coming from everywhere.

BARTIN

We arrived soon enough and went in and made our number with the powers that be. Late March now and the weather is warming up, thank goodness. The Turks don't do comfort. Managed another call to Maggie from a public call box. Does me good to talk to her. The usual wasted day on the radar. There is never any spare parts. The Turks put them in a box and hope they'll get better. Funny they'd sent a senior man from NAMSA. Mr Kandemir. He took over the interpreting. He was going to sort things. He soon discovered that some jobs are insurmountable. Sabbas spent all day chatting. It can be quite difficult, trying to do things in a foreign environment. But as I say it was a better job. We had a farewell bash. Even the Kumotan (C.O.) wanted to dance with me. Come the next day and reports handed over and I'm looking to leg it for Ankara about lunchtime. Problem. Captain Baturlap say Sabbas is a Turkish airman and will remain until cease work. I told him Sabbas belonged to me and we were bloody well going. Tell the C.O. Sabbas I say. Trouble is Turkish Officers are paramount and he never even wanted to speak to the C.O. Eventually I had my way and we left for Ankara about 14:00 arriving about 17:30 well tired and fed up. Me and sabbas had had enough of each others company and we parted not on the best of terms. Shame, I could have done a bit more for him. But we can all be selfish and unthinking. Thinking? I was thinking about the Metropole. A bath. a decent meal and a beer or two followed by an early night. Next days run for home. Having said that I decided to visit Colin and Elaine I asked Lufthansa and they directed me to B.A. for the ticket endorsement. Climbing the stairs to B.A. I espied a door with a Marconi Logo. Having got my ticket endorsed (wasn't flying civilised in those days). I banged

179

on the door of this place holding up my Marconi pass. Delight, come in! Where did you spring from? We're Orka and we represent Marconi in Turkey. I'm thinking. Why did no bastard in Chelmsford tell me? Here's a number that will help should you get into trouble in Turkey. Road accident, sickness, whatever. Still had a nice cup of tea with them and taking their number before returning to Lufthansa and booking ANK-MUN-MUN-HAN next day HAN-LHR. Got through to Colin for pick-up at Hanover. Said goodbye to the Metropole and Belma. See you next time and away. I'd been sitting in the hotel foyer reading a paper the night before, when the receptionist said to me. You should take care. Marconi has been losing it's scientists in suspicious circumstances. I, amused, pointed out that I was merely a humble engineer doing his bit. But thanks for the compliment.

FALLING-BOSTEL

Bit of a mis-start at Munich trying to reach Colin, until a kind German pointed out that you only use the 01 prefix outside the country. Eureka! Hanover and picked up OK. Elaine had come too which meant I had to sit in the back and was unable to talk to Colin. I wanted to go into Hanover and look for a birthday gift for Maggie. Finally got her a Tissot watch and a saucy Bodice thing. Perfume as always. Falling-Bostel. They had a decent flat/apartment and I'd brought him a Jade Chess set for ornamentation. We had a good night out in the Copper Kettle and dinner somewhere. Bit of time to spare in the morning. Bit of a look round and Coffee and cake before my flight. Short hop to LHR and home via Hertz by 1800hrs. Come Maggie's birthday and I give her a card and the perfume for which she was pleased. We did ourselves a bit of dinner in the evening and I put the gift wrapped watch on the table. Well pleased with her response. She thought she'd had her pressy. Jackie and David came up, Olly too and we all went out with Janine and Kevin to the Globe.

I had to present my account with Marconi. Maggie and I spent an evening on it, checking and rechecking. I started out with £4K in travellers checks. Oh and do one's own laundry. They were charging £400 a day for my services. Mean buggers. Sometimes we're given information we don't know we've got. John Azzaro on his first trip for Marconi was given the account. They were in Germany and lived in a Dutch hotel. John rendered his account in Guilders. No one noticed. So I could have put my laundry and anything else on the account. No one could read Turkish. Anyway Dave Harrison the Field service admin man called me in over a query re my account. Something about the rate of exchange claimed for the dollars I had to buy. Funny enough I'd written the rate on the back of the receipt when I bought them. I'd got it wrong and Harrison had to pay me another £20 or so when he thought I was fiddling. Trying it with Azzaro and was told in no uncertain terms. It's my account. Keep your shonk out!

MAY

I was off to Greece. Looking forward to this after the trials and tribulations of Turkey. Maggie took me to Norwich and I flew Amsterdam, thence to Athens. Taxi strike in Athens so a limo to the Marriott. John had given me his Marriott priority badge for my briefcase, of which nobody took a blind bit of notice and I had to return from my room to collect my baggage. I had a walk about next morning and found Peter Thodis the Marconi travel agent and introduced myself. John said he was good for dodgy upgrades on flights. Done John proud. I mentioned this to Peter who replied. I was hungry for business in those days but I am respectable now. Typical bloody Azzaro I thought. I was for Alexandropolis near the Turkish border and got Peter to arrange the hotel and the hire car. Ismarous was the radar station and with no Greek and no idea simply drove up the nearest mountain. I got lucky. Thought it was a fair bet. Made my number with the Greek Air Force. Very laid back after Turkey. The kit was basically running, so what was I doing there? We got on with what needed doing. The Greeks appointed each of them in turn to baby sit me and show me the sights. One of them took me to see the cave of the Cyclops. Very Small. I mentioned Helen of Troy and the love affair. He replied. Love affair be buggered. We were starving. We went for the Wheat. We had a barby on the beach and one of the officers went swimming and came back with an Octopus. Poor little sod. But they were all well pleased. Kalimari. Not for me. Usual party on finish. Marconi pay £80. Back to Athens for KLM to Amsterdam and Norwich. Home to Maggie!

ITALY

What a change I thought, a civilised country at last. I flew to Rome and overnight in the Ostia Lido, then come morn a Jetstream to Foggia. Find a hire car and drive to Vieste. Hotel Metteraneo. Rang Bryn Morgan. Your late. (Air ticket dated next day,) but I'm here now. Go find Jacontonente site. Early December. Up another bloody Mountain. Cold, wet, snow, and amazingly Pigs wandering loose. Back for Spaghetti at the only cafe I could find open. I'd lost my hat on the plane and went to buy another. Three ole boys sitting in the outfitters having a great time helping me choose. The radar was better run and the few problems they had we soon sorted out. Time I returned to Vieste the only cafe was doing Spaghetti and Cockles in their shells. Yewk! I complained to one of the Techs. Could he write for me what I wanted? Better than that he took me to their mess. Food for Africa. Lovely.

Coming up Christmas and the place is cold and wet. Hotel half closed. Breakfast being an espresso and a bit of a roll. Grimbold. A Frenchman appeared at the hotel. He was doing something else for NAMSA and wanted me to show him the route. Gladly. Follow me in the morning. I drove to site as usual and on arrival he said to me. You crazy man, you drive like you have no brakes. In this weather? I thought it was quite a compliment coming from a Frenchman. Finally job done. Run for airport and abandon car. Avis shut. Keys through letterbox and good ole BA to LHR and home.

I was down to Chelmsford after the weekend to report in and to discuss the job and it's difficulties and to hand in the account. Went up the Miami Motel and met Azzaro. He was with a couple of Jordanians. We took them up the Dukes. Nightclub. They seemed to enjoy it in spite of the music. Harry was happy to let John use the Miami. No one else on bills. A concession to Azzaro.

I had a bitch to Harry Gill, saying fed up with this job. Problem is Jim, we have no other. We have no work and the future is dead. Stick with it a bit longer. I was going back in the New Year. 17th Jan Pershembe, Bartin, End Feb Ahlatibel, March Sarkisla and finally Kutayah. I'd done Pershembe and was in a hotel at Trabson having a meal before the flight next morning and a man joined me seeing a friendly face. Glen Henry. Next morning at the airport he's asking for two beers. No response. The problem with Turkish being a phonetic language and the grammar must be right. So my. Icky Tan'a Bier to the girl resulted in two beers appearing much to Glens delight. My next interpreter was Hussein Alkan He and I got on well. He had a penchant for Fici Beer. (draught) which wasn't always available. Kutayah and it was Ramadan the Muslim month for fasting. No food on site. Come cease work would find me and he sitting in a cafe waiting for the gun to go off, signalling one could eat. I was bloody starving. A scene out of the Bible was all the people crowded round the Mosque with all the traders and snake oil sellers doing a roaring trade. Hussein and I would then retire to the Gazino and play Backgammon. I became expert. Great stuff. But again I wasn't sorry to leave. Being on one's own in a foreign country is joyless. All in all though I enjoyed Turkey once I'd got used to the place. Final thoughts. The last go at this NAMSA thing found me returning to do. Pershembe, Bartin, Merzifon.

Brian Baker who been at Dhahran with me was installing three 711 'pop up' radars along the Black sea coast at Eregli, Kefken and Karraburun. Bryn Morgan said to me. Brian needs some test equipment I'll get you to take it to him. Steady on Bryn, two inches on that map is 300 miles. O.K. Get John Mariner to meet me at Heathrow with the stuff. John was our general go-fer. On meeting John I approached the customs door and rung the bell holding out my hand for the Carnet. No Carnet and no customs man at door. Go to check-in. Excess baggage £100. Arriving at Ankara in a panic I get a porter because of the weight. Stopped at immigration. Carnet?? No Carnet. OK he say. Passport. Writes in passport. One radar system It was in reality a Signal generator. Handing back the passport saying. It leave Turkey you leave Turkey. It not leave Turkey, you not leave Turkey. And I'm handing the stuff over to Brian 300 plus miles away. In my panic I realised I'd left half of the stuff at the airport. Come the next morn and I'm at the airport and claim my 'left baggage'. No nothing to worry about. I'd left the Sig Genny at the Metropole. Flew to Trabson and a Hertz to Pershembe.

I phoned Brian at Erelgi and arranged to meet him at the Metropole at the weekend for the handover. A word with the troops re travel. Bus to Ankara. The Turks have coaches running all over. £3+. On arrival inquired about coaches back. No problem. O5:30am Monday. Sod that! Met Brian as arranged and stressed the need for me to have at least the Sig Genny back. Flew back to Trabson on Sunday. Taxi Pershembe? £30. £30? Don't be silly. It only cost me £30 to fly here. Do you want to go to Pershembe? OK £30. After doing Pershembe Brian and I met in the Metrpole again and he handed over the Sig Genny saying it was useless. Wrong Frequency band. So another £100 in excess baggage to get it back home. And smuggled past customs.

OMAN SECOND TIME

Harry called me in to his office and said. I'm putting you on a course at Marconi college on the Martello Radar of which two were in Oman. Seems to pay for the course that the Brit Liaison office in Oman was insisting on Engineers who knew the radar rather than radar engineers. So I had six weeks or so with sundry others, one of whom was Ian Pordham. He'd been on my fitters course in the RAF and was manager designate Oman. Other sections of Marconi were on the course to help share the cost. All to satisfy an ex wing commander who was the liaison officer. Then again called in to see Harry. I'm changing your lifestyle. Oman again but this time third line. Start 06:30, finish 15:00. Fridays off! Great Harry. What am I going to do Harry between 15:00 and bedtime? I'll be in the bar!

Third line was where the Omani radar equipment from the sites was repaired. Workshop, benches, stores. Bill Pekeman ran the mechanical side and Keith Saunders the electronic side. They and Shauket Ali and Bob Bedford were all accommodated at Bowshar with their wives. Our team was: Dismal Dennis Mears, Steve Black. Your truly replacing Dennis, Pete Owen, Cow eyes Connors, Steve the wireman and Andy Hawe. Andy and I joined the company on the same day. He being ex Uni. Mechanical side gave us. Filthy Firth (again) Jim Jones, Alec and Paddy Mac Namee.

Keith Saunders took the view that engineers didn't need supervision They were responsible people. They took every advantage. Never did a hands turn. Dismal did most of the work on the S600. Pete Owen on the S743. He carried a Vade Mecum because he was an electrician and self taught on radar, Marconi was paid man days in country. Bob Bedford considered it all beneath him and Andy Hawe had no intention of doing a stroke. Connors would order the most obscure part for his American equipment and sit back and wait for it to arrive, Steve Black read books. Steve the wireman only had work when asked. He read a lot. Chocolate Ali did the Locus computer repairs and was good worker. The rest used to infuriate me.

I even got sent to Masirah. Grant Stewart the manager decided Andy Hawe would go but having just returned from holiday insisted he had too much dhobi to get through. Send Parker. The mechanicals were not allowed to leave site. Bill Pekeman was the idle one. He'd put more energy into getting out of a job than the job would have taken. Having said that Paddy MacNamee was in there, and a great mate of Don's. Grant Stewart presented him with an engraved Hip Flask when he retired. Don Firth said Paddy had retired years ago. He just forgot to tell the company. His replacement Pete Nevin from Newcastle came. Sat in the bar one night, explained he was a Coppersmith by trade and was doing Oman because his son was out of work with a family to support and needed Pete's additional input. Funny or tragically he went home on leave and died. His wife said I left him in the chair with a Whisky and a roll-up while I nipped down the shop. When I came back, he'd gone and the roll-up was still burning. But we survived and the company in the mess was good. The Airworkys had one side of the bar and Marconi and BAe the bottom end. Asian bar staff. Yes I was there most nights there being sod all else to do.

I settled in to Dennis's old bench and repair of the kit. Asked Saunders why no tools? Well he say. You might steal them or flog them. That's it. Down tools. A box of tools appeared from the cupboard. Arsehole. Got on well with

186

Chocolate Ali who did all the computer repairs. Even with him in charge when Keith went on leave we were doing fine. I booked Maggie and the kids out for Christmas. Rearrange my two rooms bed wise. Worked OK. Then disaster. John Hawkins a Shams engineer wanted a change. He would take my place in third line and me his at Shams. He was looking to enjoy the delights of the Capital Area and sit on his arse in third line all day. Problem was, his Shams shift covered Christmas. Pordham wasn't amenable to saying wait until after. I was incensed and playing hardball. In the end I paid Pete Owen to do my 'shift' and borrowed his room for Tara.

Bloody Hawkins and Bloody Pordham.

Maggie drove down to Filey Way with the kids. Told them nothing. Alec ran her to Heathrow for the night flight. Poor Jan was sick most of the flight. I met them at Seeb and back to my shed. A generous two room en suite apartment. Tucked an extra bed in for Tara but of course farmed her out to Pete's place. Him being up Shams. Paddy Macnamee was organising the Falcon Mess Christmas draw. Must have been £1000 in prizes. I'd been buying tickets for weeks. Being Xmas the mess was like the Bangkok Hilton. Full of Thai wives. They all made a special fuss of Janet. Maggie became the Marconi 'wife'. Men always glad to have a woman to talk to for a change. Robert Green the admin feller had reserved me recreational transport for the holiday, so we could go out on my days off.

I had my Apple computer with me and come the draw told Paddy we'd record the winners. Typically I could have written the list before the draw. No, nary a dicky bird for us. I'd put Maggie and the kids names on my tickets to avoid the dreaded Parker no win syndrome too. Locally was the SABCO Centre a shopping complex. Janet got her ears pierced on Christmas Day. What she wanted. All the fast food people were there. McDonalds, Burger King

Hardies. Kentucky fried etc.etc. Yes the Arabs are in to fast food. Then the Souk at Mutrah. A thousand alleys full of spices and one man shops. The beach club. Place to swim and get a bite to eat. Of course there were always a few Arab men gazing at the naked female flesh as they came out from swimming. They ladies would quickly wrap a sarong around themselves. One could use the other side which was ogle free. Driving around the wadis was always good fun. Oh and the kids even got to see 'Santa Claus'. All too soon and it was over and back to Shams. And Maggie and the kids off home.

Then swipe me, they sent me to Thumrait. Short of engineers. Chance to reacquaint myself with Laverty and Blutto, Sparky had left and there were some new faces. Tony Stott who was a mechanical man and John White who was an electrician. No the company wasn't averse to sending people out as, horses for courses. Unfair to them and unfair to us who had to take up the slack. There was a lot of American equipment stored at Thumrait and it became busier than Heathrow on the build up to the Gulf War. C5's those huge transports whose wing tips nearly scraped the ground. They would fly the material in and C141's and C130's distributed it around the Gulf. Three American controllers took over the Radar cabins. They were straight off the movie screen Hank, Buck and ?? They loved our little S600 radar. (we called it Blind Pew.) The B52's would fly up from their bases in the Indian Ocean and talk to the controllers before turning round and going back. On the night of the 16th of Jan I was on nights with Pete Winchester and the B52's weren't talking, so we knew the balloon had gone up and tuned the radio in to get first reports. Great to be part of it but amazed at the awesome efficiency of man at war!

My son Colin was with the 7th Armoured and was busy dotting tanks as four hundred pieces of armour on a hundred kilometre front. Have a nice picture of him in his tank transporter. We corresponded of course. He at war and me in the background. Some kind soul in Marconi arranged for us to get GSM's for being in the theatre. Funny the day I left Thumrait to return North security discovered I never had a pass for Thumrait, but they let it pass. Once that very fast war was over and my son survived. I thought I'd like to shake the hand of the man in charge.

Back up North again and up Shams on shift. As an aside. The Radar sits in a ray dome at 10,000ft. The road up it being a scrape. A driving endorsement was required. The course being up and down the widest and gentlest of slopes. Standard routine. Talking to Dave Allton in the Falcon most nights. Then it was my turn again up Shams. While there we had a visitor and I was left to entertain the lady while the gent got the sixpenny tour. On return we shook hands and when he'd gone I asked who he was seemingly familiar. Sir Peter D' Billiere. The Brit general who had taken my son to war and brought him back. Funny how things work out. I blame the gods. He was going round the Gulf collecting gizzets from grateful Arab states.

Finishing the shift with Brian Baker and we had a storm in the night and it snowed. In Oman? Well we were at 10,000 ft. We had to rescue the guards who had walked up in their flip flops for shelter. Attempting to clear snow was nigh on impossible due to shortness of breath at altitude. We had an Omani helicopter pilot come up with supplies and warm weather clothing. And! He was at the helicopter ceiling. Bold Man!

I resigned. Wanting to be home with Maggie rather than seventeen weeks away. I was running out of time to live in the desert as a 'bachelor'. I got a job in Projects at Writtle road. Said to Harry. I can go home now whenever I feel like it. I was on leave then but Harry made me return to Oman and Shams. I flew back to Seeb and went up the mountain and did ten days shift: came down climbed on an aeroplane and flew home. Club!

CHELMSFORD

Marconi's main site was in Writtle road, A scattering of buildings being part of Comptons Light bulb works. Another across the bridge. All very secret. Research at Great Baddow and test sites at Bushey and Rivenhall. The feeling at least at Writtle road was family. One was part of Marconi and we were all happy to help. At the time they were building Martello type Radars for sites in Thailand, Greece, and elsewhere being seven in all. The specialised ISO containers were contracted out to Marshall's of Cambridge; having long past closed their own site in Gateshead. Once the first one was delivered to Rivenhall for testing they started making people redundant.

I as a projects officer was at the White gates site at Rivenhall, supposedly in charge of the place. Ray Milner as the 'engineer' was doing it his way. So we pointedly ignored each other. Don Ashmore was the overall project manager and made me responsible for the Rivenhall Inventory. All the customers equipment which was scattered over half the airfield and in various stores. Don said I'll leave my computer out and you can use that. We also had weekly meetings to assess progress and wail over the delays. The system had built in delays. Bring a Radar out and start commissioning it and then take it away for road tests, That was without and premise of any failures in the kit. i.e. If say a power supply failed you couldn't have one off the shelf. One had to be built from scratch, once all the parts had been ordered. Then assembled and tested and if it came from America then there were further delays at customs. How they ever got anything done was a miracle.

Don asked me one meeting if I'd be better at WRW Writtle Road Works pushing the parts instead of waiting for them at Riv. Well, with Twig Willis moving the kit about willy nilly as soon as I'd stored it and without reference, I thought I'll be better off at WRW. Don's final shot was. I suppose the inventory still awaits starting? Little Malcolm Thomas from Taif said. It's all in there Ashmore. Every nut, every bolt. Wind it in! Bless him!

I then found myself at a desk in projects with Doug Skinsley, Pat Stokes and Dave Driver, Basically buying parts for the Radars. Everything took for ever. Purchasing had to get three tenders for each item and then chose the cheapest, even if they had only bought the same a week ago. In the end we kept a list of surplus items left over from minimum order quantities in our 'Store' for future issue. Doug and Pat never seemed to move from their desks and Dave Driver did all his work on phones. I found walking round the factory seeing people best. Draughtsmen, label makers, Purchasers. I'd reckon I'd do a ten hour day in eight. Living in Digs and off home weekends. Then I got made redundant. Knocks one back a bit. We don't want you anymore. They sacked half the factory with the rest to follow a year later. I'll give them their due. A job shop was set up on site. We had lectures from Social Services. (basically, don't come to us. we won't accept you.) Job hunting techniques run by the local council, and two days off a week to look for work. I took everything and if I wasn't off job hunting or at home I'd be drinking coffee with Doug and Dave. I never did another hands turn. I left Christmas Eve at noon. Sad Day, Good Christmas. Sod everything. Went up to see John and Gwen. Funny thing, our land line at Utopia went wonky. No call in. One could hear ringing tones when trying but the phone remained deaf. Being Xmas. BT were in no rush to repair it and it was early Jan before it was sorted. Got a couple of calls from Projects saying Field services are looking for you. Then Azzaro rang. Harry Gill's been trying to get hold of you for days. Ring him!

Ah, Jim say Harry. Come and see me and I'll offer you a job. Conditional Oman. Well I was out of work and needed something and we knew Oman so down I went. Harry interviewed me like we'd never met. I asked if I could go back to Thumrait. He checked with Pordham, manager Oman. No problem and I signed on again. Pay back redundancy money but keep the holiday money we paid you. Which was decent of them. Then Harry loaned me out to projects while he organised my visa and no objection certificate.

First day back in projects and the boss said to me. We missed you. We didn't realise just how much work you did around here. Well swipe me. Obviously my ten hour days were all wrong. Once I sat back and did naff all they thought the world of me. They had one Radar out in Chang Mai Thailand which they were commissioning. One morning Lisa the young office girl who used to walk about half naked asked if anyone had a passport? Me I say. Good, go and buy a suitcase we want you to take out some urgent spares to Bangkok over the weekend. Once they knew I was going half the factory was round with things for me to take. And Lisa, love her said I can only get you club class on Quantas. Shame!

I faxed Maggie at Nene Fruit that I was on my way to LBFM land for the weekend. That pleased her. Good flight upstairs on a Jumbo and we landed early morning. I got through customs with my contraband and was met by Brian Baker. (Daharan). We were in the airport hotel where Brian had organised me a suite. I gave reception my ticket and said arrange for Mondays flight. Brian collected my goods and disappeared up country. I went to bed. I found a bloke called Bloomfield from systems and he said we had a car and a driver, so out shopping. Crickey. The traffic and absolute night mare, and I thought the Turks could mix it.
Back to the hotel for dinner. Boy is Thai food spicy. Come the morn and Bloomfield and I went to see the palace. We're streaming through the gates with a thousand others and the guard calls me over and said. Roll your sleeves

down. Why? A mark of respect. You've got to be joking. The rest of the visitors are in every state of undress. No matter. You! Sleeves down. The palace and the grounds were awesome. It was Easter and I visited the Temple of the Emerald Budda and said a prayer. (shoes off). Then we went shopping for Thai silk dressing gowns and fake Rolex watches. We were in the biggest department store I ever came across over eight floors. Got a couple of things and back to the hotel for siesta and drinky poos with Brian and co. They loaded me up with PCB's for repair which on arrival at LHR I declared. They are quite strict at Heathrow and I didn't want being locked up. Terry ?? projects manager was not amused.

Once back I discovered that I hadn't arranged what the overtime/travel time would be, before leaving. Too late now. Dipped out again. Visa time and Field services wanted me out to Oman fast. Sorry Maggie has a scan arranged at Addenbrooks on the day they wanted me to fly. Well do the Addenbrooks thing and get the night flight. No! I'll travel tomorrow. Being paid man days in country being the urgency.

OMAN

Hello James nice to see you. Knew you'd be back. We kept your passes. Pordham said to me. Masirah I think. Masirah? I'd arranged with Harry to go to Thumrait. Well it's tricky said Pordham but I'll ask Sandleskiv if he'll go. Odvar Skandleskiv. I'd met him at RAF Boulmer. Lovely man. loved his drink. In Oman they called him odd legs. He took Masirah for me and some years later I heard he'd died while working for the Omani Army. Shame! So down to Thumrait and swipe me Pordhams recently moved four engineers up from Masirah. What was the point of me asking and Harry agreeing on me at Thumrait? I knew and liked Thumrait. Golf course and clubhouse. Decent mess. Close to the wally camp and Salalah only 80 klicks away.

Perfect and you got your own room, en suite with enclosed garden. The trouble with Masirah was; the accommodation was crap. Being an old RAF station I recognised the billets from square bashing days. For recreation there was only water sports. There was a golf course of sorts but that was mostly shale. Hard work and hard on balls. The radars (two) sat on small hills 200 steps up. For shopping only the local wally camp. Oman is divided into Walliyats (counties). The fish factory located on the pier stunk to high Heaven. Other than that. Wonderful. I preferred Thumrait. And why not? Every other bugger seemed to get what they wanted. So after all that upheaval to get home to UK, here I was back again! Then Azzaro turned up! I rang him in the office while he was being processed and arranged a meet. Unfortunately I was on PM's and not off until nine. He'd already met a bloke up North coming down with him and had sorted a shebeen and was firmly ensconced and pissed when I found him. Why bother? He was worried about redundancy and offered to come to Oman. Harry Jumped at it of course. They were offering selected engineers two years salary to leave.

So we settled down at Thumrait. Nice to have John there, meant we had more wins on the Bingo. If he was on nights he would leave site for a drink while the other chap was sleeping. (site check he called it.) Got him on the golf course. I think he lasted six holes. Never went near it again. I did a run to Salalah shopping and happened to call in the market. Fish, Veg, fruit, and there was this enormous black woman sitting on the ground by her wares like some huge Budda. She was dressed in black with lots of yellow gold. And to my eyes so ugly she was beautiful. I asked. Can I take your photograph? No, she say. If you do you will take away my Djinn and my husband won't love me any-more. Amazing!

They did a mid life upgrade on the Radar. Digitized the receiver chain. I'd already did the same at Clee Hill for

194

NATS. They decided to use Brian Platt to manage it. Had a couple of wiremen to do the business and then commission it after. Azzaro could have done it. Or Chocolate Ali. Brian was more than nervous and of course the bloody radar never worked when it was finished. I was on days off and Brian asked me what I thought. I said I'll give you a freebie. It's the Thyraton Deck. (discharges the modulator) Nuffink. Been off the air four days. Come start of shift again and me and Butch Cassidy on afternoons. Rambo came to me and said, concentrate on getting the bloody thing working. Butch and I took the Thyratron Deck out and fixed it on the bench, Refitted it and ran the Radar up. But it didn't. Kept tripping out. Thanks to Butch's sharp eyes he spotted a crack in the Thyratron Valve, which was brand new but we changed it. Bingo up and running three hours. I went down to Smelly's bar and everyone knew. Talk about steal your thunder. That was Rambo's favourite trick. He'd ring the chief engineer after a problem saying:- we went out and I decided. Yes the we became the Royal we, and then I. He'd be telling you six months later how he saved the day when he hadn't been near the damn thing. I'm sure he convinced himself.

Peter used to get Joan his wife out. Lovely old girl. Well overweight bless her but she often invited me round for a bit of dinner. For all his faults I quite liked Peter! So with the Radar fixed and being a bit fat man-wise it was decided to put Azzaro on days so he could 'teach' the new system to people. He'd turn up ten o clockish and read a book; get a lift down when the pubs opened. Never taught sod all!

Then Marconi had a change of management and they came to visit Oman. Talking with the then manager Grant Stewart and going through the paperwork and discovering just how much John was earning. (being Harry's blue eyed boy, he had the lions share of the pay rises.) That much? What's he doing as a shifty at Thumrait. Should be in charge somewhere. John was moved to Masirah toot suite as 2 i/c much to Brian Dawsons disgust. Especially finding John in the bar when he should have been at work. Eventually he was PNG'd by a Brit controller and sent home. Usually to be sacked but he survived. Oman was worth 11 million a year to Marconi.

I was still fretting to get home, but needs must. Did get Maggie, Adam and Janet out for a visit. Tara opted to stay at home. That was when we got the phone call to say Utopia had been burgled and we flew out of Thumrait on a C-130 on Christmas Day. Normal day in Muslim land. Then the flight home. The thieves had smashed through the kitchen window by main force. Basically sorted it all out and I returned to Oman

They ran a quiz in the stiffs on a Thursday which was ever popular and people would drift off and do their thing. The golf course was closed for maintenance for Fridays competition. There was another quiz in T3 on Fridays and I could always join a team. Then a bottle draw. The trick after the bottle draw when the pub closed was to have a six pack in ice to linger over until they opened again. Have a few more and then order a take away and wander off to bed Bright eyed and bushy tailed come the morn. Riding on Azzaro's luck one week saw us in the bottle draw and the prize was a bottle of Kaiser Skul Sherry, or a closed box. Yes our ticket: take the box say John. It contained a bottle of water. Next prize was also one of our tickets. The prize? You guessed it a bottle of Kaiser Skul Sherry. Gave it to my cleaner.

Well we played golf. Shopped in Salalah. Drank too much. Watched films in the outdoor cinema. Fixed radars. Argued over the recreational transport and took leave. I resigned. Had enough. Was running out of time to live in the desert as a bachelor. We had Omani technicians we were training up to take our jobs. (their Country) Good chaps and Talal and I were buddies of a sort. As in on site but not socially. That was a no-no. Typically once I resigned I joined RS Capp. Marconi had shed most of it's engineers and advised them to join Capp which was an exclusive agency for Marconi. So we were back working at Chelmsford with no danger of being sent to Oman. Or so I thought.

I've mixed the chronology as in memory's off but no matter. RS Capp got me to go back to Oman for a three month spell. £150 a day being the sweetener. And it was Thumrait again. So pleased enough.

GREECE

Thought we'd do Greece and cover it all. I returned to Greece to do more for NAMSA. So back to Athens and this time hire a car. Saw Peter Thodis to arrange hotels. The hire car was a brand new Jetta and they asked me to organise it's first service. We were off to Volos on the Eastern side. No one particularly bothered to see me. Quite laid back the Greeks. The kit was in better order but I was largely left to my own devices. I moved hotels. The noise and the motor cycles roaring round the place. No chance!
The one I chose near the site was a Ski Lodge. A Ski Lodge in Greece? It was quiet and comfortable but of course limited menu. i.e. same, same everyday. Can't have it all! Did try the beach but after a swim, what to do? I don't sunbathe. Ah Olympus. I'll go the weekend and see the gods. A Greek said to me. There is a village on Olympus called Rapsania, where they make wine. You drink the wine: you see the gods. I did buy some but the gods must have been on holiday.

Next stop Vitsi near the Albanian border. Again up a mountain, above the tree line and with a mini cable car connecting the radar with the display and admin site. Fortunately it was Summer. I found Glen Henry's report carelessly thrown on a chair somewhere. Yes laid back. Another thing about Greece. Their bread is horrible and the string chairs which are used all over are desperately uncomfortable. Anyway next stop Athens to do Parnis. A days drive from the top end of Greece to the bottom. I made an early start for obvious reason and had a list of towns I was to pass through. I think about half way after a meal break I picked up some hitch hikers for company. Turned out the were Poles. One lad two lasses. They said they'd hitched it from Poland? Dunno but had very little English. Getting to Athens and they wanted Omonia Square. I wanted Syntagma Square. Greek traffic like Turkish traffic knows it's own laws, so I can't do it all. There I am trying to teach the Polish lad the rudiments of the Greek language so he could read the road signs for me. That was fun, but we managed it. I rack up at the Britannia Hotel in Athens and barely out the car and a policeman turns up and is going to issue a ticket. Why? Odd number cars an odd number days and even no's on even no's. Yours is wrong. I said, it shouldn't apply to hire cars and tourists. I showed him my 'map' and he agreed to give me fifteen minutes to get rid of the car, I phoned the hire people and they did the bizzo tout suite.

Peter Thodis and I dined in the Britannia Hotel that night and I arranged with him to organise my Crete stay. My next job was Parnis which is the hill behind Athens and thence to Crete and Moustakis. I'd asked Harry if I could take leave two weeks before Crete and would he swallow for a villa over the month so I could get Maggie and the kids out for a holiday. That was ok. So I'd moved to the Des Roses hotel in Kyfissia at Harry's suggestion to do Parnis. It was a short let hotel and the local cafes only seemed to do Pizzas or the dreaded Souvlaki. I did find a Chinese which helped relieve the boredom.

Come the day that I'd finished. I had all day to wait until Maggie arrived on the evening flight. Bored silly! But at last I watched her come in and we transferred to Olympic and across to Crete. A car met us at the airport and we transferred to a villa near Chania. Fridge stocked with essentials like beer and wine, Softies for the kids. The place was on the beach so was handy for the swimming and we could let the kids go themselves early as the low tidal rise in the Meddi made it fairly safe. There was a villa on the back of ours and we used their wall for exiting ours. On return one day there were new people next door. The young woman was sunbathing wearing a hat. Nothing else. Very Nice! A bit along was the Tennis Club a bar come restaurant which we used most nights. Jan Jan even had he third birthday party there. Did a run to Palehora and I'm saying to Maggie that arse is a bit big to have nothing on. Look along the beach she say. It was wall to wall flesh. We retired to another.

I did the radar at Moustakis. Distinct lack of interest from the locals. In fact it was unserviceable. Receiver faulty and no spare. They finally turned up about the last day and in a burst of Greek a fuse was replaced and the thing became truly buggered. Again not understanding the lingo. Could I stay and fix it? Sorry other jobs to do. Pete Owen said when he went there and they found he had his wife with him. Come later in the week, Enjoy Crete. Ho Hum. That sojourn in Greece cost Marconi £2500 in travel agents fees alone. Barclays bank please say Thodis. I did go back to Crete. They had another Radar at the other end of the island. That had caught fire and was waiting a repair team. What to do? Stay say Harry, earn the money. I decided on a pension rather than a hotel this time. Going for a daily DMA and saving what I didn't spend. I'd travel to the radar and check in most days but nada for the first ten days or so. What to do with oneself? Time hung more than heavy. Not so bad in the evenings when I could meet a tourist or two for a natter. Met a couple that had been running a private hotel in Luton for years and had sold up and bought a place in Colchester and while awaiting the completions were swanning around Greece and it's islands with just enough clothes to wash and wear. The repair team finally arrived and I could muck in and help. Got my time sheet signed and home again.

BACK TO TURKEY

Still doing the NAMSA work. Last lot I finished up in Cannakale (shan-ak-elle) which is on the Dardenells where the first World War debacle took place. Can't remember much about the kit but one weekend saw me across the Dardenelles and doing the Monument an embarrassed government erected. A lot of Dead. I also did the Lone Pine cemetery and a grave thus. Here lies seaman ? Seventeen years of age, his life ended scarce it had ere begun. Attaturk said of the Allied dead. They are our people now and we will tend and care for them. It was at Kaiseri that I met an old Turk whom once he'd discovered I was English was pleased to say. I fought you buggers at Gallipoli. Magic fighters. Not realising there were a lot of other nationalities involved not less the Anzacs.

On a lighter note the following weekend saw me at Troy. The 'Horse' is at the entrance and there is even a enterprising Turk selling parts of the original horse. Surprised how narrow the street were. No guide just amble round oneself. The better statuary has been set up in a museum close by, which I also visited. My interpreter this time was a young officer who never seemed to stop eating. On finishing I drove him home and was invited in to meet his family and have a meal. I had my fortune told again through the grounds of my coffee cup. Before making my way to the airport for the flight to Istanbul

My final, final visit I think was again for the 711 pop-up Radars belonging to the Turkish navy. They wanted me to go as Neil Richardson who was a shifti with me at Thumrait was doing it and I knew where they all were. Mind you there were only two working by now. One where the Turkish technician had lavished TLC on it and the other in need of the same. It was basically an oil change and cast an eye over the rest. There was much needed doing and as usual no spares available. Anything said was reported back to the Navy Authorities. Tittle tattle as in if you want one of these expensive toys: you need to look after them! For Kefken we moved in to the Crowne Plaza in Istanbul. A suite each. Beautiful food. And I put my laundry in too! Finally done all we could and reported to the Turkish Commander who repeated all our comments and said we would not leave Turkey until we had fixed the Radars. Oh! Bugger thinks I, but you cannot keep us here. Neil simply said. We need to be somewhere else, so sorry.

BELGIUM

The Belgians had decided to upgrade their ancient Radar with a 'second hand one'. The Martello's that had gone onto service when I joined Marconi in '85 were now in a military store. One was dug out and to be refurbished for the Belgium Air force. There old American one was well past it's best. There was enough Radar coverage in Europe but we all like our own. This was a long term refurbishment at Rivenhall and I got Jim Scott as the other engineer. Funny I'd seen Jim about the company from time to time. Azzaro couldn't stand him. Scott had been sent to Jordan as part of John's team and had managed to borrow John's hire car and smash it up. Usual Azzaro arrangement where he got more than he was paying for which complicated matters. So from John's assessment I was more than a little wary of Mr Scott.

We'd been on the kit a week or two and Jim was a good engineer and knew his stuff. He asked me one night to stay behind for half an hour or so. No overtime. Then en route to our digs, twenty odd miles away at Latchendon, call in the Duke's Head in Mundon. Seemed like a good idea. Seems Jim had taken a liking to me and this was the seal of approval. We made a good team and with his expertise and my quick to learn were going great guns at it. The Belgium's came from time to time to check on progress. Bringing a small sample of the local beer. More than welcome. Their visit also co-incided with the arrival of a port-a loo. That also disappeared with them. There was a loo on site but it was miles away!

Where were the training notes for the kit? This was where I would ring Tony Dennett. Ex RAF West Drayton and latterly an instructor at RAF Locking. Notes were sent to the Danes with their Martello's. In actual fact the Belgium's while assessing the Martello discovered that the Danes had digitized the training notes and had them on disk. Taking a chance they were copied, but the theft was discovered and co-operation ceased. Naughty, naughty. Like I say it was a long term job. Everything had to work, The Omani's had bought a new Martello and Al Laverty was returned from Oman along with a couple of the Arab 'techs'. One of them being Talal al Harthy, whom I'd got on well with at Thumrait. Couldn't go for a drink so showed him around 'my' Radar.

Eventually all was ready for Belgium and Jim Scott was on leave and they left me on my own to change all the contactors to 220v; being the European voltage, and thence to Belgium. We were Jim Scott and I and a wireman. All was ready in Belgium for the installation and basically we commissioned it all over again. But very quickly there being no real problems. Except one. No two! The power supply for the Locus computer had failed so we turned to the SSR to service that and it never worked. I had the absolute delight of ringing Marconi and saying, Send your man. It is broke! They sent Sermon on the Mount. Seems they changed the Secondary Radar aerial just before transhipping it for an LVA aerial and it had become full of water in a local rainstorm. Quelle embarrassment. I'd asked

Jim Mason (designer chappie) how the LVA worked and after the explanation which went right over my head I took it as read.

The routine in Belgium was to exit our apartment hotel for work. Do so. Lunch in the airman's mess 2 Euros. Work pm and down to the local bar for a Stella or two and then a meal and bed. Jim got his wife out and She: Rosemary would have a meal waiting for us. Lovely lady. They replaced me with a Marconi employee before the end. Shame, been nice to finish it. He was a full time pain in the arse and Jim couldn't stand him. Once the job was done and handed over the big party with all the hangers on over there but not hide nor hair of the engineers who accomplished the task. Sound familiar?

EPILOGUE

Going to sea was the start of my fledging. Life was good and apart from the Marsdale crowd met some nice people. Saw something of the world aside from the local dockside boozers, and ladies of easy virtue. The joining of the RAF was a turning point in life and it gave me a trade. A position in a disciplined organisation that suited me down to the ground. Man sized Radars to work on and a thorough training on the same. Lockheed Saudi Arabia was the pitts, but again I got to see the country kingdom-wide. Fascinating. The pub was a disaster but was the catalyst along with Azzaro that finally ended the marriage. Marconi was life's second wind and without it I would never have managed to restore my 'fortunes.' I've had two marriages. Got three lovely kids. Three step children. Four grand kids. Five step grand kids (if there is such a thing). Had two very dear and close friends who were my props and support. Did I need anything else? For a working class kid from Wandsworth I've had a ball! My thanks to the gods who planned it all.

James Parker Sutton Bridge. Lincs.

Printed in Great Britain
by Amazon

63608447R00118